1975

University of St. Francis
811.5 O526m
S0-BAK-444
3 0301 00027385 0

MAXIMUS POEMS IV, V, VI.

MAXIMUS POEMS

IV, V, VI

CHARLES OLSON

CAPE GOLIARD PRESS, LONDON 1968

I owe to Alfred Wegener, and Tuzo Wilson, the basis of the cover—which is of course the Earth (and Ocean) before Earth started to come apart at the seams, some 125 million years awhile back—and India took off from Africa & migrated to Asia.

Olson, September 1968

Some of these letters have appeared previously in:

Auerhahn Press (San Francisco)
Floating Bear (New York)
Jabberwock, Edinburgh
Journal of Creative Behaviour (Buffalo)
Matter, Annandale-on-the-Hudson
Migrant (Worcester, England and California)
Nation (New York)
Niagara Frontier Review (Buffalo)
Paris Review
Poetry (Chicago)
Prospect (Cambridge, England)
Set (Gloucester)
Sidewalk (Edinburgh)
Sum (Buffalo)
Wild Dog (Pocatello)
Writing 3, San Francisco
Yale Poetry Review
Fuck You, A Magazine of the Arts (New York)
Yugen (New York)

S.B.N. Cloth: 206.61560.4
Paper: 206.61559.0
Lib. of Congress No.: 68.27528

Bet
for Bet
for
Bet

For Bet

Letter # 41 [broken off]

With a leap (she said it was an arabesque
I made, off the porch, the night of the
St Valentine Day's storm, into the snow.
Nor did she fail of course to make the point
what a sight I was the size I am all over the storm
trying to be graceful Or was it? She hadn't seen me
in 19 years

Like, right off the Orontes? The Jews
are unique because they settled astride
the East African rift. Nobody else will grant
like he said the volcano anyone of us does
sit upon, in quite such a tangible fashion.
Thus surprise, when Yellowstone kicks up
a fuss

Where it says excessively rough moraine,
I count such shapes this evening in the universe
I run back home out of the new moon
makes fun of me in each puddle on the road.
The war of Africa against Eurasia
has just begun again. Gondwana

MAXIMUS, FROM DOGTOWN – I

proem

The sea was born of the earth without sweet union of love Hesiod says

But that then she lay for heaven and she bare the thing which encloses
every thing, Okeanos the one which all things are and by which nothing
is anything but itself, measured so

screwing earth, in whom love lies which unnerves the limbs and by its
heat floods the mind and all gods and men into further nature

Vast earth rejoices,

deep-swirling Okeanos steers all things through all things,
everything issues from the one, the soul is led from drunkenness
to dryness, the sleeper lights up from the dead,
the man awake lights up from the sleeping

WATERED ROCK
of pasture meadow orchard road where Merry
died in pieces tossed by the bull he raised himself to fight
in front of people, to show off his
Handsome Sailor ism

died as torso head & limbs
in a Saturday night's darkness
drunk trying
to get the young bull down
to see if Sunday morning again he might
before the people show off
once more
his prowess – braggart man to die
among Dogtown meadow rocks

"under" the dish
of the earth
Okeanos under
Dogtown
through which (inside of which) the sun passes
at night –
she passes the sun back to
the east through her body
the Geb (of heaven) at night

Nut is water
above & below, vault
above and below
watered rock on which
by which Merry
was so many pieces
Sunday morning

subterranean and celestial
primordial water holds
Dogtown high
And down
the ice holds
Dogtown, scattered
boulders little bull
who killed
Merry
who sought to manifest
his soul, the stars
manifest their souls

my soft sow the roads
of Dogtown trickling like from underground rock
springs under an early cold March moon

or hot summer and my son
we come around a corner
where a rill
makes Gee Avenue in a thin
ford

after we see a black duck
walking across a populated
corner

life spills out

Soft soft rock
Merry died by
in the black night

fishermen lived
in Dogtown and came
when it was old to whore
on Saturday nights
at three girls' houses

Pisces eternally swimming
inside her overhead
their boots or the horse
clashing the sedimentary
rock tortoise shell
she sits on the maternal beast
of the moon and the earth

Not one mystery
nor man
possibly not even a bird
heard Merry
fight that bull by
(was Jeremiah Millett's house

Drunk
to cover his shame,
blushing Merry
in the bar
walking up

to Dogtown to try
his strength,
the baby bull
now full grown

waiting,
not even knowing
death
was in his power over
this man who lay
in the Sunday morning sun
like smoked fish
in the same field
fly-blown and a colony
of self-hugging grubs – handsome
in the sun, the mass
of the dead and the odor
eaten out of the air
by the grubs sticking
moving by each other
as close as sloths

she is the goddess
of the earth, and night
of the earth and fish
of the little bull
and of Merry

Merry
had a wife

She is the heavenly mother
the stars are the fish swimming
in the heavenly ocean she has
four hundred breasts

Merry could have used
as many could have drunk
the strength he claimed
he had, the bravo

Pulque in Spain
where he saw the fight
octli in Mexico
where he wanted to
show off
dead in Gloucester
where he did

The four hundred gods
of drink alone
sat with him
as he died
in pieces

In 400 pieces
his brain shot
the last time the bull
hit him pegged him
to the rock

        before he tore him
to pieces

        the night sky
looked down

Dogtown is soft
in every season
high up on her granite
horst, light growth
of all trees and bushes
strong like a puddle's ice
the bios
of nature in this
park of eternal
events is a sidewalk
to slide on, this
terminal moraine:

the rocks the glacier tossed
toys
Merry played by
with his bull

400 sons of her only
would sit
by the game

All else was in the sky
or in town
or shrinking solid rock

We drink
or break open
our veins solely
to know. A drunkard
showing himself in public
is punished
by death

The deadly power of her
was there that night
Merry was born
under the pulque-sign

The plants of heaven
the animals of the soul
were denied

Joking men
had laughed
at Merry

Drink
had made him
brave

Only the sun
in the morning
covered him
with flies

Then only
after the grubs
had done him
did the earth
let her robe
uncover and her part
take him in

ALL MY LIFE I'VE HEARD ABOUT MANY

He went to Spain,
the handsome sailor,
he went to Ireland
and died of a bee:
he's buried, at the hill
of KnockMany

He sailed to Cashes
and wrecked on that ledge,
his ship vaulted
the shoal, he landed
in Gloucester: he built a castle
at Norman's Woe

A NOTE ON THE ABOVE

a Maximus song
the sirens sang:
he stopped his
ears with caulking
compound he listened
he travelled
he went he passed
he went in and out of wood
the bugs sang grand
birds led him on a
paradise alley (some country roads
have trees growing and the road
turns in such a way it is special,
for a few feet

the Sea – turn yr Back on
the Sea, go inland, to
Dogtown: the Harbor

the shore the City
are now
shitty, as the Nation

is – the World
tomorrow unless
the Princes

of the Husting the sons
who refused to be Denied
the Demon (if Medea

kills herself – Medea
is a Phoenician
wench, also Daughter

of the Terror) as J-son
Johnson Hines
son Hines

sight Charles
John Hines
Ol'
son /

the Atlantic
Mediterranean
Black Sea time

is done in done for gone
Jack Hammond
put a stop to

surface underwater galaxy
time: there is no sky
space or sea left

earth is interesting:
ice is interesting
stone is interesting

flowers are
Carbon
Carbon is
Carboniferous
Pennsylvania

Age
under
Dogtown
the stone

the watered
rock Carbon
flowers, rills

Aquarian Time
after fish
– fish was

Christ o Christ pick the seeds
out of yr teeth – how handsome
the dead dog lies! (horror X

the Migma is where the
Seeds Christ was supposed to pick out
: Wyngaershoek hoik Grape Vine HOYK the
Dutch

& the Norse
and Algonquins:
He-with-the-House-on-his-Head

she-who-Lusted After-the
Snake-in-the-Pond
Dogtown berries smell

as The-Grub-Eaten-Fish-Take-the-Smell-Out-of-
Air a e r the Ta of The
Dogtown (the Ta metarsia

is the Angel Matter
not to come until (rill!
3000: we will carry water

up the hill the Water the Water to
make the Flower hot – Jack
& Jill will

up Dogtown hill on top one day the
Vertical American thing will
show from heaven the Ladder

come down to the Earth
of Us All, the Many who
know
there is One!
One Mother
One Son

One Daughter
and Each the Father
of Him-Her-Self:

the Genetic
is Ma the Morphic
is Pa the City is Mother—

Polis, the Child-Made-Man-Woman is

(Mary's Son
Elizabeth's

Man) MONOGENE:
in COLLAGEN
the monogene, / in KOLLAgen

TIME

LEAP onto
the LAND, the AQUARIAN
TIME

the greater the water you add
the greater the decomposition
so long as the agent is protein
the carbon of four is the corners

in stately motion to sing in high bitch voice the fables
of wood and stone and man and woman loved

and loving in the snow
and sun

the weather

on Dogtown
is protogonic but the other side of heaven
is Ocean

filled in the flower the weather
on Dogtown the other side of heaven
is Ocean

Dogtown the under
vault heaven
is Carbon Ocean
is Annisquam

Dogtown the under
vault – the 'mother'
rock: the Diamond (Coal) the Pennsylvanian

Age the soft
(Coal) LOVE

Age the soft (Coal love
hung-up burning
under the City: bituminous

Heart to be turned to Black
Stone
is the Throne of Creation

the Black Chrysanthemum
Ocean

is the Black Gold Flower

Maximus,
to himself,
as of "Phoenicians":

the fylfot
she look like
who called herself
luck: *svas-*

tika BREAK HER up as the lumber
was broken up in the screw The mess of it astern
And the ship NOT the vessel NOT fall like dead
in the water

NO LONGER
the dead of winter be
the birth time.
THE SKIPPER

– out. Luck, out. Ling,
OUT (why was she put up with,
so long? let in,
at all? The SWASTIKA

broken up: the padma
is what was there BEFORE
one was. Is there. Will be. Is what ALL
issues from: The GOLD

flower All the heavens,
a few miles up – and even with the sun out –
is BLACK

written on Dogtown,
December 22, 1959

For "Moira"

TO HELLWITH, like
–& UP heimarmene the
warmth of Moira
the hand of Isis which
unweavest even the inextricably tangled
web of fate, assuages
any of us ("buried in us to
assuage") & puts the stars
to rights

(get up off the ass,
the ever-rutting animal hateful
to Isis

Maximus further on (December 28th 1959)

ffisherman's FIELD'S rocks with Gen Douglas lying
(having swum from Cressy's out to, with her sister) a kelp
ledge bed split when the rock cooled perhaps water
boiled it the bed of kelp for us to lie on quarter low-tide off
Hammond's

                    afternoon Manatee of my mind? Rock picture
of a beast? Lausel woman, holding out a ladle? Actually
sluggish treadle up which nature
climbed Wet white body dried Old picture Andromeda
awash Norn nurse waitress
                                        dugong
                                        crying
                                        on the rock

                              to be delivered
                              of her child
                              restored

the Impossible Rock Perseus the Husband not me

Maximus to Gloucester, Letter 27 [withheld]

I come back to the geography of it,
the land falling off to the left
where my father shot his scabby golf
and the rest of us played baseball
into the summer darkness until no flies
could be seen and we came home
to our various piazzas where the women
buzzed

To the left the land fell to the city,
to the right, it fell to the sea

I was so young my first memory
is of a tent spread to feed lobsters
to Rexall conventioneers, and my father,
a man for kicks, came out of the tent roaring
with a bread-knife in his teeth to take care of
a druggist they'd told him had made a pass at
my mother, she laughing, so sure, as round
as her face, Hines pink and apple,
under one of those frame hats women then

This, is no bare incoming
of novel abstract form, this

is no welter or the forms
of those events, this,

Greeks, is the stopping
of the battle

It is the imposing
of all those antecedent predecessions, the precessions

of me, the generation of those facts
which are my words, it is coming

from all that I no longer am, yet am,
the slow westward motion of

more than I am

There is no strict personal order

for my inheritance.

No Greek will be able

to discriminate my body.

An American

is a complex of occasions,

themselves a geometry

of spatial nature.

I have this sense,

that I am one

with my skin

Plus this—plus this:

that forever the geography

which leans in

on me I compell

backwards I compell Gloucester

to yield, to

change

Polis

is this

The River – 1

Into
In the fiord the diorite man obtrudes Obadiah Bruen's
island on his nose. Into the granite this inlet
of the sea to poke and jam the Cut and fight
the sand off and the yelping rocks, the granite
he rolls as Dogtown throws its pebbles and Merry
lay among them, busted
True inclusions
of other rocks are not commonly met with,
in the granitic material, the mass of diorite
is apparently of an irregularly circular form.
On all sides where the rocks outcrop,
it is surrounded by granitite, the two entrances
of the Reach being the only places
where it possibly have cut. These entrances
are narrow, and are bounded on either side
by granitite which is not porphyritic,
which facts almost exclude the hypothesis
that the diorite has cut the granitite.

The River – 2

the diorite
with the granite
of the Poles

– &
the
Basin
(fiord, the overlapping, both ways:

up and down and the Closed Wrinkle,

Open

she was the first one
to tear off
her girdle
to expiate
–like. The other,
who did it to make up for
what had been done to
Negroes (born
in Texas

a third for

any man,
no man
to be deprived of, as
she did take it her father was
by her mother a
cold-fucking
speech-making
political kind,
of woman. Her father
an electrical
engineer. An Engine,
her.

The Poimanderes: now I see what was up,
a year ago, chomping around these streets,
measuring off distances, looking into
records, disconsolately
making up things to do – finding myself peeing
under a thin new moon on Dogtown and noticing
rills in the March night

Dogtown the dog town
of the mother city the C-
city : METRO–
POLIS

Cashes

I tell you it's cruel. There was the Rattler, pitchpoled over Cashe's Shoals at midnight some thirteen years ago in a gale of wind, and came right side up and got into port safe with every man on board

No ship can live on Cashe's in a storm. Sailing either side a quarter of a mile and there is sixty or seventy fathom of room but right on the shoals, which is only a few rod across, the water isn't much over twenty feet deep. Only smaller vessels can go over in calm weather. It's so shallow kelp grows on top of the water and when there's a blow and the big seas come in, a hundred feet of water chopping down on the bottom, it's a bad place

The Rattler was headed along down the coast from Newfoundland loaded with frozen herring. The night was black and the captain was off his reckoning, leastways the first thing any one knew a big sea lifted the vessel and pitched her forward. She struck her nose on the bottom and just then another big one struck her fair in the stern and lifted the stern clean over the bow. Her masts struck and snapped off. With that, she went over the shoals and floated in deep water on the other side, fair and square on her keel even though both masts were broke off to within fifteen feet of her deck.

The crew of course was down below. They said it was all over before they knew what was up. They didn't sense it at all at first. They said all it was they were sitting there and then they struck the deck then came down again in a heap on the floor. They got up on deck, dazed-like, and there she was, a complete wreck.

The man at the wheel was lashed but he said afterwards when he felt her go over he thought it was all up with him. He held on for dear life and never lost his grip as he went through the water. But it's a terrible strain on a man and he was pretty nigh gone. They took him below and did all they could for him and after they got into port he was laid up for a long time. He did finally come around all right.

It was about the narrowest escape ever heard of for a vessel. They had a fair wind on the lee side of the shoal, the current was in their favor so they worked their way off and finally fell in with a vessel which towed them home.

The facts in the case are as described. The man who owned the vessel was Andrew Leighton of Gloucester, and the captain who sailed her was named Bearse.

like

Mr. Pester acknowledges his sinfulness in being at the Potter's house, saying: "I was invited by Prid et ux^{r} & Jno Stone & his wyfe & was att Stons hous from whence we weare fetched to ye Potters." Benjamin Felton deposed being at Mr. Pester's. Prid said "he was att Plimoth & it was after I came fr Plimoth y^{t} he was invited by vincen: & he was ther in my absence. Prid also witnessed it was att diner y^{t} himself invited by w^{m} Vincen." Goody Hardy deposed: "I saw m^{r} Pester his hos unfastened betweene 8 and 9 in morning & he seemed to me as if he had Laine all night ther." Goody Felton and Goody Pride also deposed. Moon rose about eleven or twelve o'clock at night. Left Goody Vincent there, and Mr. Pester and nobody else. Wm Vincen and Hary Weare left the house at eight o'clock. This was about Nov. 2.

Of old times, there was a very beautiful
woman, and she turned all heads
of men. She married,
and her husband died
soon after. She took another,
and he died. Within a single year,
she had five, and they all died, and they were
the cleverest, and handsomest,
there were. And she married, again. The sixth,
was such a silent man he passed
for a fool, but he was wiser
than people thought and he figured
to find out what was up,
with this woman. He watched her,
all the time, he kept his eye on her,
day and night.

It was summer,
and she proposed that they go into the woods,
and camp there, to pick berries. When they were in,
she had the idea he go ahead
and pick the spot and he allowed
he would, only he doubled back,
and watched her, from there out. As soon as she believed
that he was gone she went rapidly
on. He followed, unseen, until she came
to a pond among rocks in a deep wild place
in the woods. She sat down and sang a song, a great foam
or froth rose to the surface and in it appeared the back and tail
of a great serpent, an immense beast. The woman
who had taken off her clothes, embraced
the creature, which twined around her, winding inside
her arms and legs, until her body was one mass
of his.

The husband,
watched it all, saw that the serpent
let go his venom into her and that this
was what she was passing on to her husbands, to live
by transferring it to others, and he passed swiftly
to the camping ground and built
a place for the night. He laid two beds,
and built a fire. His wife came. She was in earnest
that they sleep together, he bade here sternly
to lie by herself. She laid down,
and went to sleep. Three times,
during the night, he got up
to replenish the fire. Each time
he called her but she did not
answer. In the morning he shook her,
and she was dead. They sunk her in the pond
where the snake lived.

They said she went off fucking every Sunday.
Only she said she walked straight through
the mountain, and who fucked her was the spirit
of that mountain.

A Maximus

As of why thinking of why such questions as security, and the great white death, what did obtain at said some such point as Bowditch the Practical Navigator who did use Other People's Monies as different from his Own, isn't the Actuarial the ReaL Base of Life Since, and is different From Usury Altogether, is the Thing which made all the Vulgar Socialization (Socialism CulturiSM LiberalISM jass is gysm) why I Don't Haven't Gotten it all Further?

Pound, a person of the poem

Ferrini

Hammond

Stevens

(Griffiths)

John Smith

Conants

Higginsons

Bowditch

Hawkinses

fish

ships

Lew Douglas
Carl Olsen
Walter Burke

fishermen

John Burke

houses

John White
John Winthrop

finance

wood (ekonomikos
sculpture

marine
architecture

the plum
the flower

The Renaissance a
box

the economics & poetics
thereafter

Cosmos

the
"Savage God" – Agyasta?

primitive ("buttocks
etc

the prior

DECEMBER, 1960

a coast
is not the same
as land
a coast
is not the main
a coast means
travel by horse
along beaches from
Saco south
via Ipswich to,
crossing Annisquam,
Gloucester
or by shallop
(long boat) across
Ipswich Bay
as such the Thatchers,
minister preparing to teach
Marblehead fishermen
got wrecked going
fr the settlement at Ipswich
didn't make it around
north promontory of
Cape Ann. A shore
life. At the time a frontier, woods
and Indians, Pennacooks
from Saco south, Abnaki
from Casco Bay north.
How much shore
so many fishermen
scalped, and schooners
taken, from Cape La Have
and particularly Cape Sable,
westward Fox Island,
massacre Casco, the Wakleys
south of Freeport
Arthur Mackworth
then the Gloucester founders
founding again Portland
driven out twice
and back 'home'
because Cape Ann
no Indians
after the plague:
'safe' (as wasn't
for Champlain, when 200
here, 1606 – under
Quihamenec, brother
of Chief Olmechin
of Saco: able
  Algonquin
  leaders

The same weave
of interlocking

pieces, La Have
to Dogtown in
properties sold
and cross
marriaging:

Nathaniel Wharf
whose mother was
a Mackworth
bought of Josselyn
whose mother was a Cammock
and next door on Washington
at entrance of Gee –
– or Stanwood was cut
through to make Back Road
1717 – had as neighbor William Tucker
whose grandfather was the disposer
with George Cleave of all of Portland land
direct from Gorges

or Capt Andrew Robinson
whose sister Ann
with husband Davis
of Casco Isaac
opened Dogtown
on Gee / is buried
at South Thomaston because
he fought Indians so
successfully Massachusetts
put him up
against Father Lauverjat
and French Atlantic Power
gave way and went
with Cardinal Richlieu
out of future
North American
affair

one interlocking line
was coast what Eastward
meant Eastward from
Cape Ann

force down
try out go down there
to Cape Sable
for fish to Casco
(Falmouth) to
make a new town

Ingersolls
Rider
Wakeleys
Coes

Riverdale Dogtown
proprietors
of New Gloucester

these few (1699
40 fishermen says the Frenchman
traveler (like English
on plains 19th
century making drawings
carrying elephant guns
making safari with
mountain men)

and the worst still
to come: war
with French
and Indians
all along sd coast
until Norridgewock
1724 wiped out – and Father Rasles
dead among his notes

in sd period sd schooner
invented and fishing
starts anew 100 years
after Stage Fort
(what John Winter
had made do
at Richmond's
Island Gloucester
began to make
happen, as coast
fishing
– Banks
were first born
as coast
– fishing,
to Eastward

with danger
Indians! imagine
fishing
and Indians:
William Pulsifer
of John Pulsifer
who first opened
land where
Jones Creek
turns closest
to diorite
edge of meeting
with granite
escaped home
and whenever heard
by accident someone
say Indian wld bound
off into woods and hide
for days
in shock
because
had watched
5
of rest of crew

of vessel
scalped
on fishing voyage
to the Eastward

all this
what was once
imperial
European
nations
finding
future history
from Portuguese
fishing grounds
under nose
of ice
turned
in century
to domestic
horror: farm boys
going
fishing
and ----------

----

the information of Mr Richard Yorke,
of Gloucester, taken June 22, 1713,
sayeth that on Tuesday being
the 2d day of this instant June
being at Cape Sable in a sloop
on a fishing voyage and in
a harbour called the Owl's
Head, with my sloop, and Mr
John Prince, of said Gloucester, lying
by me with his sloop, there
came down to the water side,
about three of the clock in the
afternoon, two Indian men dressed
in French clothing, with a kind
of white flag on a stick,
and called to us and desired
us to come on shore, and said
they had news to tell us and
showed a paper which they
said they had from Colonel
Vetch, at Port Royal;
and we desired them
to come on board
our vessel, and they said
they had no cause and could
not come, and after
some considerable discourse
with them, one of my men
and one of Mr Prince's
went ashore to them in
a canoe, as namely, James
Davis and Josiah Ingersoll,

who carried a gun with
them in sd canoe, and
when they came to the shore
the sd Indians came to them
and told the Indians that
it was peace; and the Indians
said, so it was, or to that purpose,
and shook hands with the men,
and said "Now Indians
and Englishmen
all own brother" they seeing
the gun in the bottom of
the canoe asked why,
for, said they "we have no
guns" and would have had
the men throw their gun
overboard. The men told them
they would not hurt them with
it. Said Indians desired
them to go on board and fetch
them some rum and tobacco. The said men
asked the Indians to go on board
with them, but they would not,
except that one of them (fisherman)
would stay on shore,
and then one of the Indians
would go on board; but
neither of these two men
were willing to stay
so they came on board
and told us that the
Indians desired to have
some rum and tobacco,
then two other of our men
went into the canoe to
go on shore – namely
Paul Dolliver and John
Sadler, and I gave them
a small pound of tobacco
to carry and give them
and had them carry
a bottle (of rum) with them,
which they did and when
they came to the shore,
one of the English,
as, namely, John Sadler
went out of the canoe
and an Indian came with the other
man on board, and as they
came the Indians kept
singing until he got on
board and when he was
got on board he said
"now all good friends", and asked
who was the skipper,
and when they told him,
said Indian came and showed

me a paper, but it was so much
worn and dusted that we
could not read it so as to make
sense of it, but supposed
it might be a pass, for the said
Indian said he had it from
Governor Vetch, and we found
in it these words, " be kind to
the Indians", and after
same Indian had been on board
a little while the Englishman
that was left on shore,
called on board and bade
us bring the canoe on
shore, and said the other
Indian would come
on board; then two
of our men as namely
Paul Dolliver and James
Davis went into the canoe
to go on shore, and when
they came off the shore
they saw two Indians
with the Englishman
and they asked them
if they would go on
board, and they said
"No", but bade them go
and fetch the Indian
on shore that was
on board, and they
came on board again
and told us that
the Indians would
not come on board,
but would have the Indian
that was on board
to come on shore.
Then James Davis
and one Josiah Lane
went to set said
Indian on shore
and to bring off the
Englishman, and as soon
as they came to the shore,
the Indian went out of
the canoe, and, as the
said Josiah Lane tells
me, they went to set the
canoe off, but the Indians
laid hold of the painter
to stop them, and the other
two Indians came and laid
hold of the painter also, and they hauled
the canoe up on shore; with that
two of the Englishmen, as namely, James Davis
and Josiah Lane, skipt out of the canoe

into the water to swim on board, but one
of the Indians came into the water and caught
said James Davis immediately and brought him
on shore, and the other two Indians went
with the canoe after Josiah Lane, and
when they came up with him one
of the Indians took his hatchet
and seemed as if he was going
to strike at him, but did not
but took hold of him and hauled
him on shore, and when they came
on shore there were several more
Indians that were come out
of the bushes with their guns,
and when they got the said
three Englishmen together they
sett them down, as said
Josiah Lane informed me,
and said they would carry them
to Port Royal

James Davis, captured

III Josiah Ingersoll,
prob. Samuel II's
son, who m. Mary Stevens
Dec 30, 1712

Paul Dolliver
m. Mary Wallis
Feb 11, 1713!
– Freshwater Cove
(died c. 1749)
cf page 87 before:
came from Cornwall direct
abt 1710

John Sadler, captured

& Josiah Lane: captured
III:
m. 1713

& Dolliver
4 of these men – Ingersoll, Lane & Sadler just married

James Davis, is probably the James IV of Squam (son of
Lieut James III
(1690–1776) who m. Mary Harraden in 1719

Maxims Letter ♯ whatever

chockablock

Once a man was travelling through the woods, and he heard some distance off a sound of feet beating the ground. He went to find the people who made the sound, and it was a full week before he came to them. It was a man and his wife dancing around a tree in the top of which was a raccoon. By their constant treading they had worn a trench in the ground, and were in it up to their waists. When the man asked them why they did it they said they were hungry and they were trying to dance the tree down to catch the raccoon.

Now the man told them there was a better way to fell a tree, a new way, and he showed them how to cut it down. In return for which he asked the skin if they had the meat of the raccoon. So they tanned it and off he went.

Another distance, in the path in the forest, he met another man who was carrying his house on his head. He was frightened at first but the man put his house down and shook hands with him, and while they had a smoke together, and talked, the man noticed the raccoon skin and asked where he got it. He told him, from the dancing man and his wife.

This was enough to get the other started. He offered him anything for the skin and finally the house. Looking it over our man was delighted to find it had so many rooms and such good furniture. But he said I never could carry it as you do. Yes, sd the man who belonged somewhere else, just try it, and he found he could, it was as light as a basket.

So he went off carrying his house until night when he came to a hard-wood ridge near a good spring of water and put it down. Inside was a wide bed covered with a white bear-skin, and it was very soft, and he was tired and he slept very well. In the morning, it was even better. Hanging from the beams were deer-meat, hams, duck, baskets of berries and maple sugar, and as he reached out for them the rug itself melted and it was white snow, and his arms turned into wings and he flew up to the food and it was birch-boughs on which it hung, and he was a partridge and it was spring.

I forced the calm grey waters, I wanted her
to come to the surface I had fought her,
long enough, below. I shaped her out of
the watery mass

and the dragger, cleaning its fish,
idled into
the scene, slipped across the empty water
where I had placed
the serpent, staring as hard as
I could (to make the snow
turn back to snow, the autos
to come to their
actual size, to stop
being smaller,
and far away. The sea does
contain the beauty I had looked at
until the sweat
stood out in my eyes. The wonder is
limitless, of my own term, the compound
to compound until the beast rises from the sea.

Maximus, March 1961 – 1

Maximus, March 1961 – 2

by the way into the woods

Indian otter
"Lake" ponds orient

show me (exhibit
myself)

The Account Book of B Ellery

vessels
goods
voyages
persons
salaries
conveyances

A Maximus Song

thronged

to the seashore

to see Phryne

walk into

the water

March 6, 1961

LATER TYRIAN BUSINESS

from
the Diadem,

"morning"
after

God the Dog,

of the 1st
Angel – who
Adores. Only after
was there a "Soul"
of theWorld – nafs
the Anima
Mundi, Bred of a Dog's
Admirer. Than which
We Are

hangs
the 7 Angels of the 3rd Angel's
Sleep – the 7
Words

as His Tongue
Hangs, dropping
Eternal Events

the Salivarating

Dog

****

March 12. 1961

for Robt Duncan,
who understands
what's going on
– written because of him
March 17, 1961

to go up & around Gravel Hill the road goes SE to
Jeremiah Millett's (which is my other kame)

and precisely by where his house was shoots NE passing,
on the north side, my personal 'orchard'
where I wrote with a crab-apple branch
at my 'writing' stand-
stump for Michael McClure (after Don Allen
and Charles Peter and David Cummings and I
ran into the pile of rotting fish – fish!
on Dogtown viz. rotting in the rills
and on Jeremiah Millett's field,
on the kame (as my life 'rotted', sd Edward Dahlberg
on my own field, assaulting my mother
because she gave me the pork chops – Edward
glaring out of his one good eye to register
his notice of the preference) "spoiling"
me – la! The which I do here record
for eternity no less, lest it be lost, that
a mother is a hard thing to get away from;
and those who interfere, in the pure sense
–Wordsworth be with me in this line,
whose Preface is a 'walker' for us all
who wld leave art and justice behind,
leave Edward Dahlberg strewn on his own
wires
The next important spot is Benjamin
Kinnicum's (fr before 1717, then five
very rocky acres, 1717) who married my
other writer of these woods and paths,
another Englishman, non-poet, John
Josselyn via his brother's son's daughter
Margaret: what a crazy early settlement
this road into the woods did have, of such
as Josselyns: John first observed (after
the strawberries all sd early colonists like Higginson
did note) he
/see below add from Josselyn\

BK's a 'hero' of my work (as, on the other – North-
road, the one went to the woodlots, I shall
celebrate Ann Robinson and her husband Samuel
Davis who settled Dogtown first of all, first
before even Kinnicum: Sam'l Davis was at
the muddy place on the N road just where it goes sharply NE towards its
2nd rise, $6\frac{1}{4}$ acres 1713: that the date
of the origin of my 2nd 'town'

Kinnicum
and Davis lie on a transverse line directly N & S of each other,
and each road beyond their respective homes
is the small areas made the life of the place
for the 50-60 years it was an overlook
of the Gulf of Maine
and the Province
of Massachusetts way down to
La Have (between La Have and Lunenberg,
Nova Scotia falls into tidal rivers
and meadows on which we saw fish
being cured 1960 as Gloucester's Meeting House
Green & estuary of Annisquam was
when fishing was to Gloucester as fishing
was to Europe, then: green fields
to dry the silver wealth in steady
sweetening sun
So small the areas are
the distances are 2500 feet from Kinnicum's
to Wm Smallmans, and 1000 feet from Widow
Davis's (1741) to James Marsh /in 1727
the North road is characterized by Joshua
Elwell's house, between the Davis house and
– what the record says – the way leading by
Joshua Elwell's to, the wood-lots, divided
1721. My problem is how to make you believe
these persons, who lived here then, and from these roads
went off to fish or bought their goods 1 mile and a half
further north, at George Dennison's store, or were
mariners – sailors – and a few farmers (though farming
was pasturing, and actually the older generation's
use of Dogtown before these younger persons chose
to live there) so far some of them went one, John Adams
was the name he took – actually born Alexander Smith
on the Backroad, was with Christian mate when sd crew
busted Bligh and sd Smith of Dogtown's people
now breed in New Hebrides –
but this is romantic
stuff I promised never to leave life riding on,
as Pegasus poetry was when Hector was not yet seen
to be cut from under muthos, lovely lying muthos
we breed again right out of our cunt-loving cock-sucking mouths,
who breed now when species has replaced man
and nature's gone away to furnaces men shoot
bodies into, and our love is for ourselves alone
I walk you paths of lives I'd share with
you simply to make evident the world
is an eternal event and this epoch solely
the decline of fishes, such a decline Bayliss,
my son calls her his first teacher, suggested
to her husband Gorton's have an aquarium
to show what fish look like – or it was already said
it won't be long, with fish sticks, pictures

will be necessary on the covers of the TV dinners
to let children know that mackerel is a different
looking thing than herrings

o John Josselyn you

"on the coast of Maine
shop-keepers there are none,
being supplied by the Massachusetts
merchants, with all things
they stand in need of;
keeping here and there
fair magazines stored with
English goods; but they set
excessive prices on them:
if they do not gain cent
per cent they cry out
they are losers. The fishermen
take yearly upon the coasts
many hundred quintals
of cod hake polluck,
which they split, salt and
dry at the stages, making
three voyages in a year"

o Josselyn you noticer

"When they share their fish
(which is at the end of every voyage)
they separate the best from
the worst, the first they call

merchantable fish, being sound
full grown fish and well made
up; which is known when it is
clear like a Lanthorn horn
and without spots, the second sort
they call refuse fish, that is such as
is salt burnt, spotted, rotten and
carelessly ordered; these they put off
to the Massachusetts merchants:
   the merchantable for thirty
and two reals a quintal;
the merchants sends the merchantable
fish to Lisbourne, Bilbo, Burdeaux,
Marsiles, Toulon, Rochel, Roan
and other cities of France, to the
Canaries with clav-board and pipe-
staves which is there and at the Charibs
a prime commodity; the refuse fish
they put off at the Charib-islands,
Barbadoes, Jamaica etc, who feed
their negroes with it. To every shallop
belong four fishermen, a master
(or steersman), a midshipman,
a foremastman, and a shore
man who washes it out of the salt
and dries it upon hurdles pitcht
upon stakes breast high and tends
their cookery; they often get
in one voyage 8 or 9 £ a man for
their shares; but it doth some of them
little good, for the merchant, to
increase his gains by putting off
his commodity in the midst of their
voyages and at the end thereof,
comes in with a walking tavern,
a bark laden with the legitimate
blood of the rich grape which they bring
from Fayal, Madera, Canaries, with
brandy, rhum, the Barbadoes strong water
and tobacco; coming ashore he gives them
a taste or two, which so charms them that
for no persuasions that their employers can
use will they go out to sea, although fair
and seasonable weather for two or three
days, nay sometimes a whole week, till
they are wearied with drinking, taking ashore
two or three hogheads of wine and rum
to drink off when the merchant is gone. . . .
When the day of payment comes
they may justly complain of this
costly sin of drunkenness for their shares

will do no more than pay the reckoning;
if they save a quintal or two to buy
shooes and stockins, shirts and wastcoats
with, tis well, other-wages they must
enter into the merchants books for
such things as they stand in need off,
becoming thereby the merchants slaves
and when it riseth to a big
sum are constrained to mortgage
their plantation if they have any"

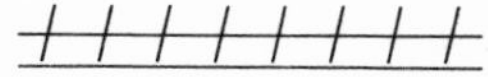

Further Completion of Plat

Lt James Davis 14 acres 1717 and to share 4
more 1728/9 with his son-in-law James
Stanwood – all on the east side of the lower
road, defining therefore that stretch: the first
10 acres, May 23, 1717, are "of land and Rocks
between Joseph Ingarsons and Bryants."
Ingarson Ingersoll, and Bryant tied, as
Smallman, and James Stanwood is to be,
to Falmouth (Portland's) rearising

James Demerit,
the other later surviving one, with Ingersoll,
on the E side altogether – to Smallmans –
married Mary Briant and seems therefore
(as James Stanwood) to have come on,
as the fishermen and mariners did, to take over
earlier pasture uses of this higher land
up above Mill River. For, besides James Davis
his brother Ebenezer, and James' own son Elias,
also had acres, intermingled with John Day's
and Ezekiel Days',

and as the Days, but
as ship-owners, at the head of Mill River the Davises
were, like Captain Andrew Robinson, evidence how
quickly fishing came up in the 1st quarter of
the 18th century. And flushed their children
into Dogtown. Ebenezer died in 1732 leaving £3047
and Elias, coming on so fast the guess is he
was to be the strongest man in Gloucester, died
at 40 and already at sd age was worth

£4500

with a wharf at Canso (a fishing room);
and 6 schooners,

John, Mary, Molly, Flying Horse
& 3/4s of Greyhound and Elizabeth

[More on Joseph Ingersoll
to follow; and on the other side of the lower road,
Deacon Joseph Winslow, who bought from his father-in-law
Day, in 1724

A Prayer, to the Lord, cast down like a good old Catholic,
on the floor of San Vitale, next to Dante's tomb, in the
midst of the mast/bast of the construction

so I can get on with it,
my great White Cadillac driving through Dogtown

March 28, 1961

fr Cape Sable into the stream in
Gloucester Harbor in 14 hours
& 25 minutes – the Nannie
C. Bohlin September 30, 1893,
225 sea-miles or average of
15½ knots per hour. Under
both topsails, & each sail rove
flat as a yacht's

<u>Bohlin 1</u>

Bohlin 2

Bohlin
hove to, once
loaded down
with pickled herring,
in barrels – & with more
lashed on deck:

all having breakfast
with their boots on
from the boards
being sprung: Mr Bohlin

did not believe in a vessel
until her 3 inches of oak planking
is loosened up

imagine if Bohlin had sailed
the Lady of Good Voyage
or his own Bohlin instead
of Dr Stimson's in
the ocean race

he'd a rolled down a hill
in a snow storm
to arrive at the bottom
where his vessel was moored

Gee, what I call the upper road was the way
leading by Joshua Elwell's to the wood-lots
1727

and Cherry or the lower road was, 1725, the way that
leads from the town to Smallmans now Dwelling house

B. Ellery Cinvat Bridge aer

the winning thing

what did Stevens do if he didn't make ships? as late
as 1667, when signing the oath asked of all Americans then
to pledge allegiance to a new English king, Stevens
is listed as ship carpenter

no 'wharf' as such
is known to have been his

tho his descendents
all come to play a leading part in the
life of the Harbor – especially his great-
granddaughter Susanna who became the mother
of David and William Pearce – Stevens,
tho the leading citizen, is all over the
Cut: was, then, the "Beach" his
private graving yard? or did he
build at all? The question has
that power in it, that previously to coming
to Gloucester this man had built the largest
ship then known in England – and had been
so desirable Spain's spies had sought to
buy him, as they had earlier tried to John Hawkins

he would have lived a life as large as
John Winthrop Jr also refused

but even colonially
Stevens dwindled, on the face of the record
I'm not sure he did He lived here on the front
of the city 40 years, until the day
he ran away, age 70, to wherever he
did go

The question stays: what did he
do? did he contract vessels for out of
Gloucester? what was ship-building, if
Stevens did build, to bind his coming to the later act
of Andrew Robinson – or Ingersolls and
Sanders? It stays, that not after so much
of a break in time, the type of vessel
which changed fishing from that point on
was built or invented in Gloucester

One wld say, not out of thin air.
1713, a schooner. 1693 Stevens dies,
a ship builder. In those 20 years the
Ingersolls the Sanders and Robinson are
continuing ship building. Was Stevens not the
head of something – the winning thing –
got hidden all the years?

Bailyn shows sharp rise
shipbuilding Gloucester: in 1706
its production amounted to 17.3
per cent of the registered vessels
and 12.8 per cent of the tonnage
produced in that year by towns in the
Bay Colony whose names were specified

But these are not her fishermen: average
tonnage is 46.4: the schooner

                        or then still
called 'sloop' or ketch (William Baker,
1962, is of the opinion
what Robinson did do, 1713 was
to fit the long known two-masted fore-
and-aft rig – the Dutch fore and
main mast combination – to
a typical ketch hull (though Gloucester records

1702 show Nathaniel Sanders buying twelve trees,
and they to be oak of the town, for the sloop he is building,
and the same year, December, his brother Thomas building
likewise a Sloop for the Parsonses.

23 School and 16 Columbia:

myrtle and violets. and wood.

---

the bottom
          backward
(of
    the sea (grounds

fish eat on   cod bred in winter in

Massachusetts bay, went off shore

with spring   then Georges with winter

again

            ice had dropped

Banks in the water, kame of the bottom, fish orchards and gardens,

                                                            tenements

messuages of the billions of generations of halibut paralleled

settlers' lives

                        where fish go, after

and Danish cylinders now descend to measure

paleontological times when figureheads from East India brigantines

sat in formal gardens so that old maids held their stomachers

running as girls on Pearce Street

                    the Atlantic is a bottomed

Pacific

              I stand on Main Street like the Diorite

stone

Jl 17 1961

as John Burke
read the comics
at the City Council
table saying
when you guys have played
long enough there's no use
of my wasting my
time: brains
are not to be
wasted

'okloloidoros

Letter 72

of love & hand-holding sweet flowers & drinking
waters) Hilton's & Davis', Davis' the

garden of Ann

↘ get back to & Elizabeth & Eden

Nasir Tusi & where I fall

man is the fallen angel

and after Davis' swamp – Joshua Elwell

sitting high in heaven

→ Bennett placed himself

above 75′

Hilton above the trough between

(on the edge of 75′ too)

– & Sam'l Davis on the height of

the next rise, inside 125′

(100′ lying almost exactly the middle

of the 600 foot distance between his

& Hilton's houses); and Joshua Elwell

the other rise on the Commons Road,

or "to the wood-lots" (1727),

on the other

side of the 2nd trough, at

125′ Thus

three 'hills' or hogbacks

& two brooks

characterize the upper

road (as against the lower

or dog Town road proper,

where moraine, and the more

evident presence of rock-tumble
gives the road, & center, its
moor character – moonscape
and hell) the Commons is
garden, and manor, ground rose
                                                  & candle
shapes of spruce & bayberry garden

The View – July 29, 1961

the arms
of Half Moon Beach,
the legs
of the Cut

Descartes soldier
in a time of religious
wars

a map of Dogtown: St
Sophia, Fishermans /
Field, Fishermans /
2 acres on which to dry

cod via
racks
in a field
like snow
fences or tables
at a lawn
party

& ladies
in boots
who wear
coifs to keep
the sun from burning
their necks

The Shoreman, Sunday Sept 10
1961

In the interleaved Almanacks for 1646 and 1647 of Danforth

1646, August	1.	The great pears ripe.
	3.	The long apples ripe.
	12.	Blackston's apples gathered.
	15.	Tankerd apples gathered
	18.	Kreton pippins, Long red apples, } gathered
1647, July	5.	We began to cut the peas in the field.
	14.	We began to shear rye.
Aug.	2.	We mowed barley The same week we shear summer wheat.
	7.	The great pears gathered.
Sept.	15.	The Russetins gathered and Pearmaines.
1648, May	26.	Sown 1 peck of peas, the moon in the full. Observe how they prove.
July	28.	Summer apples gathered.
1646, July	20.	Apricocks ripe.

(as in footnote in
Winthrop's Journal

ta meteura

meteor things

after the weather the
meteors

parsonses
field

Thurs Sept 14th 1961

Elicksander
Baker,
on the River Bank Above
Done Fudging 16–
THIRTY-FIVE
and to:
FORTY-FIVE, his age
28 to 38, and having
by wife Elizabeth in those years
5 children – certainly the earliest
known births Gloucester (except for
Conant children, Woodbury? Balch?
Stage Fort 1623/4 to 1626/7 –
Alexander, born Done Fudging Jan 15, 1635/6
(the father and mother had arr. Boston
in mid-summer, aboard the Elizabeth
& Ann, Capt. Roger Cooper, with
two first children, Eliz age 3 and
Christian age 1) thus Alexander Baker
II possibly 1st child Gloucester
among the persons of the incorporation
of the Town;   Sam'l,
born January 16, 1637/8;
John, June 4, 1640;
Joshua [from whose blood Ethan
Allen] born Gloucester April
30th, 1642 – just about
day Endecott & Downing divided
Gloucester up – and Hannah
September 29, 1644: sometime
after her birth and before
October 4th, 1645 (date the
mother & father are admitted
Boston Church) the Bakers
sold out, at Done Fudging, to
George Ingersoll, from Salem
(Ingersoll was still in Salem date
his father's will, 1644)

One has then
a placement:
a man, & family,
was on the River,
just above the Cut,
by 1635. And for
10 years. Also probably
his neighbor Stephen
Streeter may have
been there that
early? In any case

as goodmen
Baker & Streeter
the two get referred
to in jointure the
moment the Town is
found; and, curiously,
their adjoining
property is
picked up from
them by another
pair equally
holding together
Gloucester
for similar
10 years, Ingersoll
and Kenie, though
each leave
Done Fudging quickly
for the Harbor:
each is possessed
of a front
on Fore
street,
& the water, by
1647 (Dec.

Baker thus fixes
occupation of Cape
during least known
years between
1st settlement and
incorporation
as Osmund Dutch
does the 'fishermen'
of the Harbor front:
his letter to wife Grace
is – from Cape Anne as
nauta or sailor –
July 18th, 1639

and Abraham Robinson
Thomas Ashley (whose
property Widow
Babson bought up
at his bankruptcy
1642) and Willm
Browne show
– via shallop –
as down there
on the Harbor
before June
1641 – and "fishermen"

specifically
[Thomas Lechford,
Notebook, page
406]

Add Wm
Southmeade
or Southmate
as possessing
Thompson fishery
stage Duncan's
Point and
therefore probably
here as early
as Dutch (and
Thomas Millward AND
you have a handfull
who are the hidden
handfull from which fell
the later life as though
they were . . .
yes:

Elicksander
Baker
goodman
Streeter
Osmund
Dutch
William
Southmate
Thomas
Millward
Abraham
Robinson
Thomas
Ashley
William
Browne

& definitely the ministerial student Thomas
Rashleigh, traveling
from the Divinity School which
Harvard college was 1639
to hold service on
Curtis Square
(where
R R
cuts between
Burial Ground and
hill) so
more parsons by
Baker and
Streeter?

– and other fishermen
at head of Harbor
Cove :

FILL
Harbor
and
River
FILL

quiet
few originally
experiencing
what we have each
differently
known – like the mocking bird
drove me hard (mocking
me? if he mocks 28
different sorts of
song does a mocking bird not also mock
the living person? such curiosity
must
extend
to looking in on
the secrets of
my cabinet as well
as the songs of
his companion
birds) like the mocking bird
last night
in the slow coming in
of the fog – a hot
night such the creature a
mocking bird is – loves
heat, and night – no mocking bird
was here
1635 1639 1907 was
accidental visitor
from the south
Mimus polyglottos

But by 1920
had increased so
was becoming almost
authority Dr Townshend
a resident – and at all times
of the year F B Currier
found them nesting (at Newburyport)
in 1914. Four young
grew to full size. A
second
pair nested
the same year. In 1915
two pairs also
nested;
one
in 1916;
and two
in 1917

Of the Parsonses

I pick out
the Garden, the Spring the well
of George Henry's division with
his brother the
flat stone by a cherry tree

the Garden Nathaniel's, deceased
when Samuel fisherman alias coaster
sold it to Ebenezer tanner abt
19 rods of land called the
Garden

1732

SWly to
a Plumb-Tree. The well

exactly opposite the Morse
house, on the westerly side across
from the middle of it, 1 acre of
rocky ground where said Solomon
Parsons house stands, and is bounded. . . Excepting
Mr John Parsons' land where his well is & there
to bound by sd land as it is and no way to infrindge
on sd well privileges, Eliezer & wife Mary, May
1736/7

Mr John Parsons orchard Gravenstein
russets Greenings and Northern
spies in the complex westerly
of the Morse house with the well
and the spring – the "Spring House"
the Leach's now winter home was summer camp
I went through today with Stewart
and Mrs Leach, when Walter Cressy
was selling water after he'd blown up
the rock vein and dried the Parsons
spring, to get his own a Cressy-
Strong strongwayWalter and Neal,
and Bertha, living it up with a pony
a goat a sheep a Labrador retriever while acquiring
more & more of the old Parsons
woods and ledge fronting over the
Cut like Frontenac bearing
down:

greensward
is a light of the fall of ground
may not be the like of light
coming off water but land's
fall causes feeling to run as
spirit does from sea & sky, she
said at 10 in the morning she
felt she was her mother meaning my

body was hers I went to
the mirror to look if it was
me and called her, on the phone,
she joshed me and it was that night
when she went with Josie Boone
to see the Chocolate Soldier she
was struck by a taxi getting off
the street car and Josie was so
scared she didn't find out what
hospital they took her to – 12
hours of premonition had not known
before & never knew again

Spring land leads from the S end
of the Morse house (across the street)
in, 8 rods W'ly it says from
the house there a line to begin
fr the rock to a great rock by
the Spring which is abt 10 poles,
leaving the Spring common, thence
NWly etc

THE BEGINNINGS (facts

Dutche mariner New England coast & transport England to
Bay 1632 – along with John Gallop who
ran his pinnace back & forth to
Ipswich

Babson guesses Robinson might have come across from
Plymouth 1631

1633 anyway Rev Eli Forbes says (1792) on authority
"Vide ancient Mss" persons here and met to carry on the worship
of God among themselves – and sung psalms

THE BEGINNINGS

old Englonde   new England
1636 old John (White) to new John (Winthrop) urgeng
"to sent on for fishing
which is the first means that will bring
any income into your lande

halfe a dosen good boates masters
& three or foure good splitters talks John
who hath known fishing since early Dorchester
Company days – now getting on 13 years agone

1637: the longer you defer fishing &
use other means that may bring you in some
supplys the more
you weaken
your body & will ere longe
etc

Hugh Peter pushing 1639 – sd year Gl.
gets going: stages builded nautas turning
fishermen (Dutch example
Millward another – young Gallop maybe

March 1640 Craddock
shoving at Winthrop

& then with war
England civil war & West Indies open
further to Yankee
Trade come Gloucester
into
Being : April SIXTEEN
Forty-two

On Bemo Ledge he fell
one dark night – and didn't
crawl up out of that one
in his red Jacks, the pet child
of the lucky sea

THE CUT

March 13, 1638/9

to view, whether it may not be
cut through

December 10, 1641

that they that cut the beach between
Cape Ann & Annisquam
shall have the liberty to take sufficient
toll, for 21 years

Scheria – ?

island
(near Miletus, &
below Scamander?
on the River –
Hercules
or Athena, balled
headed clerks etc hauled
hair via hair rope
the statue into
place

Oct 18, 1961

My Carpenter's Son's Son's Will, Lt
William Stevens, 1701, Inventory 1712/13

. . . .

a certain previledged place
call the Cutt where   34 – 10 – 00
vessels pass through for money

comparison (for value)
house sawmill barn
74 £

Maximus, at the Harbor

Okeanos rages, tears rocks back in his path.
Encircling Okeanos tears upon the earth to get love loose,

that women fall into the clefts
of women, that men tear at their legs
and rape until love sifts
through all things and nothing is except love as stud
upon the earth

love to sit in the ring
of Okeanos love to lie in the spit
of a woman a man to sit in her legs

(her hemispheres
loomed above me,
I went to work
like the horns of a snail

Paradise is a person. Come into this world.
The soul is a magnificent Angel.
And the thought of its thought is the rage
of Ocean : apophainesthai

roared the great bone on to Norman's
Woe; apophainesthai, as it blew
up a pool on Round Rock shoal;
apophainesthai it cracked as it broke
on Pavilion Beach apophainesthai

it tore at Watch House Point

II

apophainesthai
got hidden all the years
apophainesthai: the soul,
in its progressive rise

apophainesthai
passes in & out
of more difficult things
and by so passing
apophainesthai

the act which actuates the soul itself –
she loomed before me and he stood
in this room – it sends out
on the path ahead the Angel
it will meet

apophainesthai

its accent is its own mirage

III

The great Ocean is angry. It wants the Perfect Child

October 23rd and 4th
1961

brang that thing out,
the Monogene

the original unit
survives in the salt

Going Right out of the Century

I, JohnWatts, via
Thomas Morton, claimant
to possessing disposal
of lands & islands of
sd coast including
Gloucester Harbor, did take
salt stored on
10 Lb Island by
ship Zouche Phoenix, London

& did not disturb
shallops thereon lying
as well as other
fishing gear – sd salt
in tunnes for use in
drying fish was
all I took, the
provenance of same being
sd Morton declared

in his hands & skipped
I wld suppose with
value received
I herein testify

Nov 19, 1961

V

A Later Note on Letter # 15

In English the poetics became meubles – furniture –
thereafter (after 1630

& Descartes was the value

until Whitehead, who cleared out the gunk
by getting the universe in (as against man alone

& that concept of history (not Herodotus's,
which was a verb, to find out for yourself:
'istorin, which makes any one's acts a finding out for him or her
self, in other words restores the traum: that we act somewhere

at least by seizure, that the objective (example Thucidides, or
the latest finest tape-recorder, or any form of record on the spot

– live television or what – is a lie

as against what we know went on, the dream: the dream being
self-action with Whitehead's important corollary: that no event

is not penetrated, in intersection or collision with, an eternal
event

                The poetics of such a situation
are yet to be found out

January 15, 1962

128 a mole
to get at Tyre

"View": fr the Orontes
fr where Typhon

the 1st to navigate
those waters
thus to define
the limits
of the land: Helen,
said Herodotus,
was only the last
of the European girls
to be absconded with
by the Asiatics

for which read
Phoenicians,
Semite sailors

Along those extending lines (rhumbs)
there was Manes first (Minos
maybe) there had been
Gades there was Pytheas
out into the Atlantic

far enough up into the North
for the Atlantic to be known

Portuguese
are part Phoenician (?
Canary Islanders
Cro-Magnon

Islands,
to islands,
headlands
and shores

Megalithic
stones

Stations
on shores
And Sable

Then England
an Augustine
land

January 15, 1962

The Young Ladies
Independent Society
of East Gloucester
has arisen
from the flames:

the Sodality
of the Female Rule
has been
declared: We will Love
with Kisses

Each Other; and Serve Man
as Our Child

I

patriotism
is the preserved park
of ▬▬▬▬
Magnolia pirate,
and Oliver Viera
his First Mate

II

Ralph Harland Smith at least
thinks that his intelligence
was given him by nature
or his mother or father for
some use which he at least
has tried
to use it for

▬▬ ▬▬
borrows it it is clear from
some one else

▬▬▬▬
it is clear
thinks nature
is an ambulance

III

the wild life
CREW
of the Nancy Gloucester Elspeth ▬▬▬
and the former head of the Harvard Business School
and the Brookline
lawyer
the NANCY GLOUCESTER'S ahoy

boys – at least Mr Brown
of Old Magnolia
made a pass

Bk ii chapter 37

1. Beginning at the hill of Middle Street the city
which consists mostly of wharves & houses
reaches down to the sea. It is bounded
on the one side by the river Annisquam,
and on the other by the stream or entrance
to the inner harbor. In the Fort at this entrance

are the images of stone and there is another
place near the river where there is a seated
wooden image of Demeter. The city's own
wooden image of the goddess is on a hill
along the next ridge above Middle Street
between the two towers of a church called
the Lady of Good Voyage. There is also a stone image
of Aphrodite beside the sea. 2. But the
spot where the river comes into the
sea is reserved for the special
Hydra called the Lernean monster,
the particular worship of the city,
though it is proven to be recent
and the particular tablets of Poseidon
written on copper in the shape of a heart
prove to be likewise new.

the rocks in Settlement Cove
like dromlechs, menhirs
standing in the low tide
out of the back of the lights from Stacy Boulevard
at night

out of the back of the light,
from Stacy Boulevard on the water
at night

my memory is
the history of time

Peloria the dog's upper lip kept curling
in his sleep as I was drawn to the leftward to
watch his long shark jaw and sick brown color
gums the teeth flashing even as he dreamed.
Maximus is a whelping mother, giving birth
with the crunch of his own pelvis.
He sent flowers on the waves from the mole
of Tyre. He went to Malta. From Malta
to Marseilles. From Marseilles to Iceland.
From Iceland to Promontorium Vinlandiae.
Flowers go out on the sea. On the left
of the Promontorium. On the left of the
Promontorium, Settlement Cove

I am making a mappemunde. It is to include my being.
It is called here, at this point and point of time
Peloria.

November 12, 1961

In the Face of a Chinese View of the City

on what grounds shall we criticize the City Manager?
or the D PW ?   as easily as we do
the Superintendent of Schools for the texts
he buys?   for the snow left on the streets
so a car slews and a boy has a broken
pair of eyes?   for the insufficient time the City Clerk
spends on the earlier records of the City
even if like dog-licenses, and births and marriages,
he is up-to-date on the latest
of the suit-clubs and the bowling alleys? Business is obviously
cant and social life almost entirely
liberal but public office, as forever,
remains distinct – and moral – or
the life of the individual dwindles into
stink – a man in his own kitchen boiling
paregoric is he then and there on an open line to
the vein of the police, and invadable as such, by what
term ? Cant mores praise accomplishment
obvious competence clear management of
$5,000,000 a year's receipts for ex-
penditures leaves open what judgement
if the color of the lights on the Main
Street turn the lips of women blue
and all days are cheery too
with the smiles of windows washing clothes?

The few,

and the masses, as though they constituted
possible public life – while those who lead them
are as cherry-red after golf or shoveling
their sidewalks clean as Santy Clauses hung from silver wires
fat or lean dirty or clean, the differences
of Santy Clauses not by any tally measure for what is what
the single probity public figure better be
what had he better be?

January 5, 1962

while on
Obadiah Bruen's Island, the Algonquins
steeped fly agaric in whortleberry juice,
to drink to see

Shag Rock,
bull's eye

& gulls
making such a pother
on the water in the sun
I thought it was Round Rock Shoal
in a south easter

Τὰ Περι Τοῦ 'ηκεανοῦ

A 'learned man' sd Strabo (meaning Pytheus:
the Greeks
were the 'English'
of the Mediterranean,
as the Germans
were the Romans

had rushed up into the White
Sea – & "travelled all over by foot"–

And did it all with limited means and in a private
capacity /Tanais! itself

Cyprus
the strangled
Aphrodite – Rhodes

Crete
– the Mother Goddess
fr Anatolia
Phrygian Attis

Malta: Fat Lady

Spain

Jan 17 1962

after the storm was over
out from his cave at Mt Casius
came the blue monster

covered with scales
and sores about his mouth
flashing not too surely

his tail but with his eyes
showing some glare
rowing out gently

into the stream, to go
for Malta, to pass by
Rhodes and Crete

to arrive at Ireland
anyway to get into the Atlantic
to make up a boil

in northeastern waters
to land in a
grapevine corner

to shake off his cave-life
and open an opening
big enough for himself

Jan 17 1962

to travel Typhon
from the old holdings

from taking the Old Man's
sinews out and hiding them under

the bear rug, from Sister
Delphyne

who listens too easily
to music, from Ma

who is always there
and get that building up

at the corner of
Grapevine Road & Hawthorne Lane

with Simp Lyle
for manager

up the steps, along the porch
turning the corner
of the L,

to go in the door
and face the ladies
sitting in the comfortable

chairs,
and greet Simp
with the morning's mail

January 18, 1962

people want delivery

When I used to stop to talk to the Parenti Sisters
or Susumu Hirota, the McLeod sisters

who ran the Harbor View
would call up the post office
and ask what my truck was doing
at the corner of Rocky Neck Avenue

the coast goes from Hurrian Hazzi to Tyre
the wife of god was Athirat of the Sea
borne on a current flowed that strongly
was taken straight through the Mediterranean
north north west to Judas waters
home to the shore

Jan 19 (Friday) 1962

3

tesserae

commissure

Jan 19th 1962

Lane's eye-view of Gloucester
Phoenician eye-view

1833 14 october 443 Vessels at anchor in the harbor besides what Lay at wharfs

Older than Byblos
earlier than Palestine
and possessed of an alphabet
before the Greeks

round about the pawl-post
the heavy lines are wound
which hold by the chocks
the windlass when wound

from running back

CHRONICLES

1

As Zeus sent Hermes
to draw Agenor's cattle
down to the seashore
at Tyre, date

1540 BC, and thereby
caused the pursuit
of him by Agenor's
sons – one to

Carthage, one to the edge
of the Black Sea, one
to found Thebes,
another

to establish the rich
gold mines of Thasos –
meanwhile Zeus
as an immaculate

white bull with one
black stripe down him
has caught Europe
up on to his back,

his softness
fooling her,
she placing flowers
in his mouth,

he sails off
to Crete, near
Ida, and there
also Phoenician

persons are
born, Europe's
sons Minos,
Rhadamanthys,
Sarpedon

2

Taurus,
King of Crete,
caught Tyre
when Agenor

and his sons
were rallying

from a sea-
battle,

and plastered
it – the Evil Night
of Tyre John Malalas
calls it,

when Cretans
took everything
and blasted her
back in to the sea

from which
she came, when
Ousoos the
hunter

was the first man
to carve out
the trunk
of a tree

and go out
on the waters
from the shore

These
are the chronicles
of an imaginary
town

placed as an island
close to the shore

Sanuncthion lived
before the Trojan War
a self-conscious historian,
then, existed in,
and as of Phoenicia,
before 1220 BC
(or 1183). The details
of the Parian Chronicle
and such matters as
two Hercules, a
Phoenician Melkart-
Hercules more than
5 generations previous
to the Greek Hercules
(born 1340 BC,
by the Parian Chronicle)
make sense

which loan-words
& other epigraphical
matters now available
enforce: that the Libyans
and the Phoenicians (Agenor
was said to come from Egypt
& to be the son of Poseidon
by Libya – who herself
was the daughter of
the king of Egypt) one
sees a hub-bub
of peoples – Indo –
Europeans,
Libyans (the least known
of all sources of
serious inroads on
Egypt & collaboration
by the Libyans with
the still unknown Raiders
of the Sea) – and Uganda:

is there anything
to the possibility
that some of the non-Euclidean
roughnesses are here
involved – Hittite, or Hurrian
may not be the only evidences,
there may be East African
– and again what about Libyan?
movements to the center
of the 2nd Millenium:
Semite Sailors? They may be
Gondwannan creatures
who swung off,
for market
from the Eastern Edge

(where did the Sumerians
come from, into the Persian
Gulf – sea-peoples
who raided and imposed themselves
on a black-haired previous people
dwelling among reed-houses
on flooded marshes?

John Watts took
salt – and shal-
lops, from
the Zouche Phoenix
London's supplies
10 Lb Island

3rd letter on Georges, unwritten

[In this place is a poem which I have not been able
to write – or a story to be called the Eastern End of
Georges, about a captain I knew about, as of the days
when it was important to race to market – to the Boston
market, or directly in to Gloucester, when she had fresh
fish, and how this man had such careful charts of his
own of these very shallow waters along the way
to market if you were coming in from the Winter Cod
Grounds on the Eastern End – the point was to cut the
corner, if you were that good or that crazy, though he
was as good as they come, he even had the charts marked
in different colored pencils and could go over those
rips and shoals dug out in a storm, driving a full-
loaded vessel and down to her deck edge, across them
as a wagon might salt licks or unship her wheels and
ferry across – it is a vision or at least an experience
I make off as though I have had, to ride with a man
like that – even have the picture of him sitting on
his cabin floor following those charts like a race-
sheet while taking the calls down the stern passage-
way and if it sounds more like Henry Ware & Paul Cot-
ter in the Eyes of the Woods, it could be so, for I've
looked & looked for the verification, and the details
of sail at a time when there were no engines – and I
went to James Connolly expecting to be able to depend
upon him, but somehow he hasn't come across, or it's
all too prettied up, and it was either Bohlin or Syl-
vanus Smith or it may have been someone as late as
Marty Callaghan but the roar of this guy going through
the snow and bent to a north easter and not taking any
round about way off the shoals to the north but going
as he was up & down dale like a horseman out of some
English novel makes it with me, and I want that sense
here, of this fellow going home]

THE GULF OF MAINE

Altham says
they were in a pinnace
off Monhegan
season
1623, having left
Cape Anne

and trove
mightily
until in
Damariscove Harbor they
split up
in a storm

the sides
of the vessel
with the current running North North East
were ground
in turn
by the same rock wall the vessel

switching about
like a bob and his wife
and Captain's Bridge's, in London
reached by mail via
Plymouth's agent

address
High Court Row and St by Chancery Light

could not have imagined
had they known,
that night,
their husbands

were on such a shore
and bandied
as they were: 4 men
alone, of all of them,

dragged themselves up
in the early morn
out of the wash
of that dreadful storm
so many chips among ground timbers

of what was left
of the pinnace. Such was the coast
when sturdy oak-built 17th-century
little boats out of London and Plymouth
cast their nets, King James said We do approve

of the Pilgrimes going
to the sand shore of
Virginiay
if fishing is
the holy calling

they go there
about, dear James for corfish
did they go Madame Altham
Madame Bridge
called on James Shirley

one bright City morning
for pounds and sterling
sturdy pence
in recompense
of their dear husbands

so. The night
was growley
the waves
were high the high built pinnas
tossed the winds down
pressed

the Little James
until she was far spent
& fore went head down
into the sea below the
waves her sticky masts

with thick crows nests
were up above the
waves and broken-stumped
wild balls of fire
played over

where their heads
below the water
filled and shoes
and coats pulled down
the crew

and Captain Bridge
& Mr Altham swam
like underbodies going by
in an outrageous park

or film until
their knees
were smashed
on small rocks
as their poor pinnace likewise poorly lay

chawn mostly but some parts of her bruised sides
now resting on the sands where we shall
dig them up and set them upright as posts
at just the signal place for tourists
to come by and not give one idea

why such odd culls
stand along a fishing
shore
though not used much at the present time
and mostly well-dressed persons
frequent it

existed
3000
BC?
from
Red Sea, via
Bahrein? /

Poseidon
(Samothrace?

Taurus
the beetle
stuck in his
leg

Minos
Megiddo
Jericho
Sarpedon /

Rhadamanthys
Europa
Dardanus?
(Electra?
Atlas /

and Zeus?
name-wise
derivation

Cabiri the 7
great planets
(things? the
'great gods'
meaning?

Additional "Phoenician" notes

phalaropes
piled up on Thatchers

(struck in the night
of September 2nd, 1899

and 800

to 1000 of them

killed themselves

against the lights between

12:30

and 4 A.M.

Aristotle & Augustine
clearly misunderstood Anaximander
And in doing so beta'd
themselves

off-upland
only Ubaid
gets "in"
to riverine
(Squam

Old Norse/ Algonquin

Sunday June 17, 1962

VI

The earth with a city in her hair
entangled of trees

And now let all the ships come in
pity and love the Return the Flower
the Gift and the Alligator catches
–and the mind go forth to the end of the world

HĖPIT·NAGA·ATOSIS

entwined
throughout
the system,

they saw a Serpent that lay quoiled like a cable
and a boat passing with English aboard, and two Indians
they would have shot the Serpent but the Indians

dissuaded them, saying

that if He was killed outright they would all be in danger
of their lives (upon a rock at Cape Ann, Josselyn, Rarities
Discovered in Birds, Fishes, Serpents and Plants, London

1672

Barbara Ellis, ramp

the diadem of the Dog
which is morning
rattles again

They brawled in the streets, trapped the night watchman

with his own stick, made such an uproar

the Bay itself was notified and Endecott

had to apologize that he hadn't yet brought them

under his control

DEEREST SIR, I heard nothing further of Glocester
business till the 3d day of this week at even, when
I received a letter from Mr. Blinman, together
with a complaint of the towne against Griffens
companie for severall misdemeanours, And
at the foot of the complaint a reference
from your selfe and 3 other Magistrates to
mee for the redress of them. I therefore despatched
away a messenger betimes the next morninge with
a letter to Mr. Griffen, that hee would sende me

such of his crew whose names I had under written his letter, to answer to the misdemeanors of Sabbath breaking swearing and drunkenness If they did resist or refuse, not to strive with them nor to use any provoking termes, but to take witness of their cariadge and to returne mee an answere; which here I have sent you inclosed. I would have proceeded against them according to your former directions (to wit) with force: but I had rather if you see good try first an other way, which is to send a prohibition, under your and divers of the Magistrates hands besides forbidding Mr. Stephens and the rest of the ship carpenters there, or any other within this Jurisdiction upon some penaltie, not to worke a stroke of work more upon Mr. Griffens shippe till they had further order from the governour, etc. I desire therefore to heare from you what you would have done

Mr. Griffin presented for swearing by the name of God
Mr. Philip Thorne, mate to Mr. Griffin, presented for swearing and drinking to excess.
John Hodges, Stephen White, Edw. Bullock and Anselm Whit presented for swearing, and fined 10s. each.
Richard Hedges presented for swearing and abusing the watch, and fined 15s.
John Bruer presented for swearing and drunkenness, and fined 1 li. 10s.
Mr. Philip Thorne gave bond for all.

out over the land skope view as from Alexander Baker's still
stonewall orchard pasture land-bench over the River looking
to Apple Row and the Sargents other side the scoop out of
the surface of the earth a lone woman sat there in young
skirt the gulls use it in early morning to drop mussels
on the low-tide rocks

Dogtown to the right the ocean

to the left

opens out the light   the river flowing

at my feet

Gloucester to my back

the light hangs
from the wheel of heaven

the great Ocean
in balance

the air is as wide as the light

Hesiod said the outer man was the bond with which Zeus bound Prometheus

the illusory
is real enough

the suffering
is not suffered

the foreknowledge
is absolute

Okeanos
hangs in the father

the father
is before the beginning of bodily things

Part of the Flower of Gloucester

from the sunsets
to the rubbish on the Harbor bottom
fermenting so bubbles
of the gas formed from the putrefaction
keep coming up and you watch them break
on the surface and imagine the odor
which is true
at low-tide that you can't stand the smell
if you live with Harbor Cove or the Inner
Harbor to your side

Veda upanishad edda than

Wrote my first poems
and an essay on myth
at Kent Circle
at Kunt Circle

there was a Dance Hall there
like literally ye Olde
West on the spot whar he
looked out and saw the sun gleaming
on the snow after
the St Valentine Day's
Storm spring
1940

exactly
300
years
writing
at the stile
before
the town
age
29

where Cunt Circle
was to be where the inverted triangle
of the road
went around
Steep Bank Hill

eating packages of peanut butter
sandwiches
bought from
Peter Anastas's Boulevard Sweet Shop the Bridge
as far as I chose to go in the February air

Went off to New York
by the Boston boat
as soon as the work
was over wearing
going through the Canal
an Arctic cold weather
completely smothering
upholstery fabric
hair mattress
headgear with eyes only
protruding

until I couldn't stand
the god damn thing and went out
on deck
with my head
itself

the 1st lot from the Cutt

lying next to the stile

the sea added

I am the Gold Machine and now I have trenched out, smeared, occupied
with my elongated length the ugliest passage of all the V
running from the Rest House down the hill to the
Tennis Court, the uncontaminated land which of all Stage Fort
does not bend or warp into new expressions
of itself as De Sitter imagined the Universe a
rubber face or elastic bands falling
into emergent lines from which string the crab-apple
tree is a dollyop on the lawn of the Morse house over
Western Avenue

Through the grate in a door of a cell
inside which about where the Rest House is another man
and I were I had then in my hand a wooden page or block
with tissue covering its face in which two jewels one
of which a long red drop and I wished
so strongly to show right away to Robert Duncan
and another who were walking away down the V and shot it
into the space of the door which it exactly fitted
and they turned, and saw it, and went on and taking
the block out of the window stuck my fingers vertically
through the same hole or grating and waved by moving
my fingers at them where they were towards the Tennis Court

The land was relieved. I had drawn my length all this way
and had covered this place too

In the harbor

Can 9 Nun 8

Nun 10 Can 11

Charles Olson

Friday November 23rd

#1

Kent Circle Song

at My Aunt Vandla's
village a carbuncular
(goiter) gambrel
and Federal
all frilled with lace
and a gold brooch

at their throat

a silvered handle
in the door
and the walls
all made of cake

and into the oven with her

I swung out, at 8 or 10
waking to the bedroom wall
and the sweet smell of toilet soap
in the house at Wellesley Hills

in the 3rd floor bedroom
of the

JW (from the Danelaw) says:

They don't know they spoil – and from the beginning.

and as those words go down they set free, he
is non-referential in that moment this John Winthrop
had as a leader Vedic
senses he was a magistrate
in the mixed rule   the people
were the liberty   the ministry
were the purity – Hebraic

and the civil, which Winthrop was, was
authority. 1593 Arisleus'
Vision was published Basel
to make sure that what was known was
passed on to posterity viz that the planting

shall be
        on the widest possible
                ground

Fri Nov 23rd

proem

the Algonquins had cleared the land there, Champlain
shows Stage Fort as containing five wigwams with
crops, it was the first place the English as fishermen
Westcountry men used to settle on, importing
the large company house in which the original
14 men lived, the first stage was built
there, it was divided among 17 men
in 1642 as – what they were – fisherman's
field, and the Parsonses made it their
village or homestead from shortly thereafter
until my father's time – and mine
when it was 'Barrett's' so far as we
were originally concerned
he building his first summer camps
about the time he was Mayor of Gloucester (1914)
on the model of his sister Lizzie Corliss's
henhouse – in fact the first one was
a hen house the one the bed broke down under
my mother & father the first night we came to Gloucester
slept in, and with the rain
which I had seen
out Johnny Morgan's Candy Kitchen window
the afternoon previous,
continuing through the night my mother
had had a lot of Gloucester already
and never ceased
remembering

We shifted around thereafter
were up on Bond Street
with Bill Collins the letter carrier
another summer
and at the Morse's the next
and for some summers had the gambrel,
the old schoolhouse of the Cut
which Ed Millet has had now for years
But my father was always planning
to get back up on the front
and when the big camp
was maybe first built
we had it from then on forever
fronting out on the Park
exactly at the stonewall line
of what was probably always
a certain division of fisherman's field,
that the edge of the cultivatible,
or usable sun and air edge
for salting and drying fish,
was that line which goes in angles with some strictness
from the Cupboard to the low spot of Western Avenue
opposite the marsh
– the old stream

which now backs down the new houses
on the marsh side and is a mess where the Strongs
have kept horses since they were Cressys
and tar trucks and broken-down road
equipment were since Homer was also
(later) superintendent of streets, for years
and Roland had the oil & hop-top contract and
the two brothers
who owned the American Oil Company courted
the two beauties of the camps
– & one walked away with the darker

the brook, coming out of the forest,
at just about Bond Street
at 1 mile from the City
flowed then by John Parsons
orchard, and well, made James
Parsons house a dell (see
Bertha Cressy's mother's painting
of the old Cressy homestead, just there)
and Jeffrey the original wampum
of the tribe, the buck and founder
his house which George Ingersoll
had owned and before him George Norton another
ship's carpenter had built, the first
house settler after the Algonquins
(and the Dorchester Company house, which was probably
up in the field over Settlement Cove like a fortress
or Christopher Leavitt's at Portland on an island
to have room around it and sight in an enemy
country on shore
– this is a precis
of land I am shod in,
my father's shoes

not the intaglio method or skating
on the luxurious indoor rink
but Saint Sophia herself our
lady of bon voyage

(Friday
November 23rd
♯ 6)

mother-spirit to fuck at noumenon, Vierge

ouvrante

(A Prayer to Our Lady of Good Voyage

Sunday November 25th

1962

Monday, November 26th, 1962

and his nibs crawled up
and sitting on Piper's Rocks
with a crown on his head

and looking at me with a silly grin
on his face: I had left him out
of my monuments around the town

I

he who walks with his house on
his head is heaven he
who walks with his house
on his head is heaven he who walks
with his house on his head

II

she who met the serpent in the pond the adulteress
who met the serpent in the pond
and was kissed
by him was wrapped in his
coils

she had to die if she could not pass, by fucking,
the poison
on if her husband would not fuck with her
and die if by fucking she could not get rid of the
poison after
she had fucked with the king of the pool

III

  the woman who said she went out every Sunday
and walked right through the rock of the mountain

and on the other side she said she was fucked
by the Mountain

        all that, was her joy
every day of the week, and she was the happiest
of the tribe,

and that was her explanation, given by her, of why

and that was how it was she was
so happy

November 1962

into the Stream or Entrance to the Inner Harbor, Gloucester

the Inner Harbor also known as the River, Gloucester

on the other side of the River, Gloucester

the Head of the Harbor, Gloucester

at the place where   Dutches Sloo drained in

THE FRONTLET

into the light
of Portuguese
hill Dogtown

Dogtown's
secret
head
& shoulder

    bull's shoulder

lifting Portuguese hill into the light

the body
of Dogtown
holding up Portuguese hill into the light

Our Lady of Good Voyage sitting down on the front of the
unnoticed head and body of Dogtown secretly come to overlook the City

the Lady of Good Voyage held out there
to keep looking out toward the sea
by Dogtown

                        the Virgin

held up
on the Bull's horns

THE CITY
(OF GLOUCESTER

December 9, 1962

Homo Anthropos

– and Our Lady: Potnia,

and Poseidon (Potidan

[Theroun]

Thursday January 10th 1963

to enter into their bodies
which also
had grown out of
Earth

Mother Dogtown
of whom the Goddess
was the front

Father Sea
who comes to the skirt
of the City

My father
came to the shore
the polyphony
came to the shore

he was as dust
in the water
the Monogene
was in the water, he was floating
away

oh I wouldn't let my Father
get away

I cried out
to my Mother
"Turn your head
and quick"

& he came
to the shore
he came to the
City

oh
and I welcomed
him

& was very glad

The Cow
of Dogtown

Shaler says
On Dogtown Commons
several of these areas (he is speaking of the
stratified elements of glacial accumulations
which, he has just said, generally do not rise
more than sixty feet above the sea level
[that is, now; he has already of course
made it clear that at the time the glacier
was over the land the land mass itself
was depressed from its present level by
at least double the 65 feet; which
makes it necessary to add, that, at
that same time the sea itself was 'out'
– drawn up as vapor which had else-
where formed the ice – to a depth by which the Banks,
for example, off-shore, were themselves – like
these Dogtown Commons – deposits of good
top-soil carried from other places in the feet
of the ice and only finally left – as
Dogtown and the off-shore Banks – when
the wall of the last ice began to give way)

He continues:

These elements (of glacial
accumulations) are hardly traceable in
any continuity above the level of 40
feet; but at a few points they extend
in an obscure form nearly to
the summit of the great moraines
[an example the 'top' of Dogtown,
via the Upper Road, where one comes out
(missing the Whale-Jaw) on an upland
or moor which must be about like
the barrow Bob Lowrie thinks is
a covered Viking ship
and burial. The top of Dogtown
puts one up into the sky as free-
ly as it is possible, the extent of
clear space and air, and the bowl
of the light equalling, without at all
that other, false experience of mountain
climbed, heaven. One would sit here
and eat off checker berries, and blue-
berries in season – they are around
the place, at this height,
like cups and saucers, and one moves around to
eat them, out of one's hands,

not by getting up but going from
place to place on one's own behind. Burning
balsam, or the numerous bushes of bayberry
one could stay here with the sky
it feels like as long as one chose; and
there is enough wildness, or profiles in
the rocks, the inhabitation of their shapes,
to supply plenty of company – none of the
irritation and over-presence of nothing-
nesses which makes woods, or any
place else than the kame meadows of
Dogtown and this bold height of
it, not as interesting. Shaler says: "On Dogtown Commons
several of these areas of kame deposits
were during the period in which this
district was inhabited brought into
the state of tilled fields, and now
appear as small pasture lands destitute
of boulders."

[This is of course identical
with Stage Fort Park, of which the
highest point is exactly Shaler's statement
of the highest of such deposits – 65′]

"These high-lying benches of stratified drift
material," he continues, "probably
indicate points where small subglacial
streams emerged during the process
of the retreat of the ice, bringing forth
a quantity of detrital matter and
depositing it upon the surface of the
shoved moraine at a time when the
mass lay below the level of the
sea."

On to this kame
on to this shoved moraine
when the ice moved off
or was melted

And the land came up
and the sea rose
to the beach levels it now assumes,

and the sky
was as near, as,
at the top of the long slow rise
of either of the Dogtown roads

[or Hough avenue – or the path
from the Barrett's more steeply up to the
crown, now that Ray Morrison has cleared
away Lizzie Corliss' hen house the Barrett's
backhouse Lizzie's sad pear trees

Viola's true rubbish heap flower garden]
the far sky is as near as you stand,

Nut is over you
Ptah has replaced the Earth
the Primeval Hill
has gone directly
from the waters
and the mud
to the Cow of Heaven
the Hill stands
free

She leans
from toe to tip of hands
over the earth,
making the Cow-sign
with the earth

(she is the goddess
of earth and heaven and sea)

one could live in the night
because she has to do with it,
encompasses it
in the day on Dogtown the day
is as close as the sky

her air
is as her light
as close
one is not removed even in passing through

the air, moving around, moving from one place
to another, going even across the same field

Nut is in the world

(Monday February 11th,
1963

15 3
autobiog.

Stage Fort Park

an ice-plug a wherry where I hid my car a nights a fucking
and they tell me this was a gore under ice where the rocks made a whirlpool
when the land was then depressed below the level
of where the sea now is but the sea was out and here
in the hole of Stage Fort Park forty feet further down and then let up was the bed
of a Merry mac as wide as Massachusetts

the earth was down from the weight of the ice upon it
and great beds of water flowing under carried detritus
was my kame and those hollows and the rise
of choke-cherry trees I have eaten my father
piece by piece I loved my cannibalism

of the cake and flesh I now have windings of as steep and left-ward twisting
as those ice-rock grindings were
the giant river ran over and caught
where ground itself is a fucking hole

Further Completion of Plat (before they drown   Hist. of Glou –

Dogtown with a reservoir, and beautify it)

Lower Road, Kinnicum, before 1717, Joseph Ingersoll and Bryant houses above him
by 1717, and Smallmans up at the end before 1725: eight
or possibly ten years to 'settle' that

Upper Road, earlier: Samuel Davis (where reservoir probably won't reach),
1713, William Hilton where reservoir will be (in swamp directly sheared
off him) before 1719, Elwell next above (on Hilton's side) 1719
– the upper end – and all of it for sure by Jabez Hunter, 1725

So, on the outside, Dogtown established 1713-1725, twelve
                                                                        years

                              The division of wood-lots was 1725-6 – and the
statements, which lock both roads up, are these:

1725 (Lower Road) "by the way that leads from the town to
Smallmans now Dwelling house";

and – 1727 (Upper) "the way leading by Joshua
Elwell's to the wood-lots"

                              In the expanding period of Gloucester (and the nation)
directly after 1703 (3rd generation of settlers
  –Malthus' evidence on population)

        – 'set' by 1725, & living up through 1775
(when B. Ellery

        etc

Saturday February 16 1963

Sequentior

Smallmans definitely there 1721 [action of committee on
wood-lots at first report, Dec 19 1721]

Thus spread, of time, on Lower Road
probably 4 years all told, for it to be occupied to the end.

These were the 'marrying years' of most of these men. Thus
in their twenties.

And the Reverend John White, who had been their Pastor,
is on the record (letter to the General Court,
on their behalf, 1740) that
                                                  "the Petitioners are most of them
Seafaring Men

February 22nd, 1963

Licked man (as such) out of the ice,
the cow ——— did who
herself came into being
so that Ymir would have some source
of food (her milk one supposes

Odin was born of either this man directly
or one generation further on, Odin's mother
was the giant ——— .

157

<u>Gylfaginning VI</u>

a cow Audumla,
which had come into being to provide food
for Ymir, licked a <u>man</u> [not a
iotunn] out of ice whose name was
Buri, whose son (or maybe it was Burr himself)
Burr (or Borr) is the father of Odin

Heaven as sky is made of stone (Diorite – ex-
granitite) Tartaros's threshold at least
is made of a metal native to itself
And Earth
  – is made of grout

All night long
I was a Eumolpidae
as I slept
putting things together
which had not previously
fit

the Vault
of Heaven,
from which the rains
spring

            all the horns of the cattle
particularly the deformed horns
come upward to carry the impression to
Ptah

                    Ptah,
the man of the earth. Over the earth
is the Dome
of the sky "deformed"
by the sea, terminated
by the exercise
of holes.

turn out your
ever-loving arms, Vir-
gin And
Mother

                    Vulgar
swamp And cow
or sow. Wetlands.
Juice. And in the triple-force
dripping

Orge

"at the boundary of the mighty world" H. (T) 620 foll.

Now Called Gravel Hill – dogs eat
gravel

Gravelly hill was 'the source and end (or boundary' of
D'town on the way that leads from the town to Smallmans
now Dwelling house, the Lower
Road gravelly, how the hill was, not the modern usableness
of any thing but leaving it as an adverb as though the Earth herself
was active, she had her own characteristics, she could
stick her head up out of the earth at a spot
and say, to Athena I'm stuck here, all I can show
is my head but please, do something about
this person I am putting up out of the ground into your hands

Gravelly hill 'father' Pelops otherwise known as
Mud Face founder of
Dogtown. That sort of 'reason': leave things alone.
As it is there isn't a single thing isn't an opportunity
for some 'alert' person, including practically everybody
by the 'greed', that, they are 'alive', therefore. Etc.
That, in fact, there are 'conditions'. Gravelly Hill
or any sort of situation for improvement, when
the Earth was properly regarded as a 'garden
tenement messuage orchard and if this is nostalgia
let you take a breath of April showers
let's us reason how is the dampness in your
nasal passage – but I have had lunch
in this 'pasture' (B. Ellery to
George Girdler Smith
'gentleman'
1799, for
£ 150)

overlooking
'the town'
sitting there like
the Memphite lord of
all Creation

with my back – with Dogtown
over the Crown of
gravelly
hill

It is not bad

to be pissed off

where there is *any*
condition imposed, by whomever, no matter how close

any
quid pro quo
get out. Gravelly Hill says
leave me be, I am contingent, the end of the world
is the borders
of my being

I can even tell you
where I run out; and you can find
out. I lie here
so many feet up
from the end of an old creek
which used to run off
the Otter ponds. There is a bridge
of old heavy slab stones
still crossing the creek on
the 'Back Road' about three rods
from where I do end northerly, and from my Crown
you may observe, in fact Jeremiah Millett's
generous pasture
which, in fact, is the first 'house'
(of Dogtown) is a part of the slide of
my back, to the East: it isn't so decisive
how one thing does end
and another begin to be very obviously dull about it
I should like to take the time to be dull
there is obviously very much to be done and the fire department
rushed up here one day – they called it
Bull Field, in the newspaper – when just that
side of me I am talking about,
which belonged to Jeremiah Millett
and rises up rather sharply
– it became Mr Pulsifer's and then,
1799, the property of the town
of Gloucester – was burned off.
My point is, the end of myself,
happens, on the east side (Erechthonios)
to be the beginning of another set
of circumstance. The road,
which has gone around me, swings
just beyond where Jeremiah Millett had his house
and there's a big rock about ends my being,
properly, swings
to the northeast, and makes its way
generally staying northeast in direction
to Dogtown Square or the rear of
William Smallman's
house where rocks pile up
darkness,
in a cleft in the earth

made of a perfect pavement
Dogtown Square
of rocks alone March, the holy month
(the holy month,
LXIII
of nothing but black granite turned
every piece,
downward,
to darkness,
to chill
and darkness. From which the height above it even
in such a fearful congery
with a dominant rock like a small mountain
above the Hellmouth the back of Smallmans is
that this source and end of the way from the town into
the woods is only – as I am the beginning, and Gaia's
child – *katavóthra*. Here you enter
darkness. Far away from me, to the northeast,
and higher than I, you enter
the Mount,
which looks merry,
and you go up into it
feels the very same as the corner
where the rocks all are
even smoking a cigarette on the mount
nothing around you, not even the sky
relieves the pressure of this declivity
which is so rich and packed.
It is Hell's mouth
where Dogtown ends
(on the lower
of the two roads into
the woods.
I am the beginning
on this side
nearest the town
and it – this paved hole in the earth
is the end (boundary
Disappear.

[MAXIMUS, FROM DOGTOWN – IV]

a century or so before 2000
BC |
| the year rebegan in
March |
| festival days
of wild untamed undomesticated hence wild
savage feral (Father's
Days our father who is also in
Tartaros chained in being
kept watch on by Aegean-
O'Briareos whose exceeding
manhood (excellent manhood
comeliness
and power – 100 or possibly
to use the term of change (with
the reciprocal 1/137 one of the two
pure numbers out of which the world
is constructed

(the other one is
'Earth' mass mother milk cow body
demonstrably, suddenly, *more*
primitive and universal (? Hardly

The problem here is a non-statistical
proof: Earth 'came into being'

extraordinarily early, #2
in fact directly following on
appetite. Or
as it reads in Norse
hunger, as though in the mouth
(which is an occurrence, is 'there',
stlocus)

that the Earth
was the condition, and that she
there and then was the land, country
our dear fatherland the Earth,
thrown up to form a cairn, as spouse
of Uranos: a i a

the original name
of Colchis (cld be a 'local'
reference, that the Great Name
the Earth shall have been
Kuban where those
inventors of the Vision – the
Civilizers – were
'local'? some sure time prior to
2000
BC
/ the statistical
(stands)
outside
the Stream, Tartaros

is beyond

the gods beyond hunger outside

the ends and source of Earth

    Heaven Ocean's

Stream: O'Briareos

helped out by Poseidon by being given

Cympolea, P's daughter, for

wife sort of only superintends

the other two jailers of those

tied up in

Tartarós – and those two,

[in other words below below – below

is a factor of being, underneath

is a matter this is like the vault

                you aren't all train

of Heaven it counts

if you leave out those roots of Earth

which run down through Ocean to

the ends of Ocean as well

the foundations of Ocean

                – by Earth's prompting

and the advice of Heaven, his grandparents, this person

Zeus put the iotunns those who

                        strain

                      reach out are

                        hunger

put em outside (including the last

the youngest child of Earth

her last one, by love of Tartarós,

by the aid of Love as Aphrodite made
strength in his hands and untiring
feet – and made of all the virtues
of Ocean's
children – snakes a hundred heads
(a 'fearful "dragon") dark flickering tongues
the eyes in his marvelous heads 'flashed
"fire", and fire burned from his heads,
when he looked (at the enemy or
as Shakti was shooting
beams of love directly
into the woman he wanted to be
full of love) and there are 'voices'
inside all his dreadful heads
uttering every kind of sound (imaginable?
unspeakable HughWhite says Hesiod
says (not to be voiced?
    for at one time they made sounds
  such as solely the gods
  caught on to
but at another Typhon
was a bull
when letting
out his
nature, at another

    the relentless lion's
heart's sound

and at another sounds

like whelps, wonderful to hear
and again, at another, he would hiss
so the sky would burn

they threw him
into his father's
place it would take you one year
from the tossing in this direction and that before you got
to its pavement, Tartarós lies
so thoroughly out 'below' but 'outside'
(having nothing whatsoever to do with
gods or Earth's . . . but suddenly
a 'loss' has been suffered: Tartarós
was once 'ahead' of
Heaven was prior to
(in coming into being) this 'child'
of Earth: Tartaros
was next after Earth (as Earth
was next after hunger
itself – Typhon
was her child, by Tartarós, even if last
as Heaven was her child, first

The step back, to the seam
of the statistical Nebel
and "End of the World" out of the union of which
by what occurrence was before

hunger – it is like Ocean
which is 9 times around
earth and sea (Heaven is 9 times

around earth and sea folding and folding
earth and sea in its backward it

wraps and wraps the consistency
of mass in until the stupid story
of earth and nature is lent
what in its obviousness and effort it
can't take time for, and makes its stories
up, temporality sifts
out of Ocean out of Ocean was born
                                                                        3000
(when his wife was Tethys)
daughters —— Tartarós the 'prison'
beyond the gods and men beyond hunger
and the foundations of Ocean
are a seam: Cottus and Gyes,
with whom Briareos is the third 'guard'
have their dwelling
                    ep' 'Okeanoio 'Themethlois
the lowest part the bottom tithemi

Θe

        Ocean deems
himself

On that edge or place
inverted from Ocean starts
another place
Tartaroś in which all
who have been by the statutory
thrown down or overthrown, are
kept watch on Night and Day
(Night's house is right over
their heads, in which one door
Day goes out when her mother
comes in and neither
are ever together at the same time
'at home' – Hell is just over
their heads
and so is the 'way-up', Bifrost
(Styx's house and Iris the messenger are
bungled prettinesses of this way
this marvelous ladder the
color of all colors
back where the gods, and appetite,
and so is the way out for them,
for these imprisoned original
created – all of the first creations
of Earth and Heaven (or of Ocean and Tethys
all these instances forwards of except
the official story

Heaven himself the 2nd, Kronos
who acted for his mother in de-maleing
his father
is in Tartaroś
away from all the gods

while the glorious allies of loud-crashing Zeus
Cottus and Gyes, and o'Briareos
guard them

Typhon
is in Tartaroś,
threatening as he did (as they had,
the last to give the gods a scare
who would have come to reign over mortals
and immortals

the heat took hold on the dark-blue sea
when Typhon and Zeus engaged
Hell trembled, where he rules
over those who have come to him

and the iotunns before Typhon
locked up in Tartaroś swung
from the clangor and the Earth
shaking

he burned all the marvellous heads of the monster
and conquered him and lashed him
and threw him down in his mother,
who groaned

and a great part of her melted
as tin does from the heat of him blasted
where Zeus had tossed him

and then in the bitterness of his anger Zeus
tossed him into Tartaros

The life-giving earth
had crashed around in burning
the previous time when all the land had seethed
and Ocean's streams and the sea
had boiled – and it was this 'lava'-
like which had undone the earlier
Giants because they were Earth-born
Earth's own meltedness had burned
their underpinnings and
defeated them, against Zeus's
stance
Cottus and Briareos and Gyes
had done that day, of the Civilized War,
their turn – for the Boss

with their missiles added to his
'bolts' they did their co-evals in, and
were the ones who chained them

(as the Theogonia poet says,
for all their great spirit, their
metathumos

There it was, Tartarós
which had been there as early as hunger
or at least directly after hunger & Earth
and before Love
Yet Love
in the figure of the goddess born
of the frith from her father's Heaven's
parts accompanied Tartarós
– as Night had Heaven the night
his son had hurled off his parts

Love accompanied Tartarós
when with Earth in love he made
Typhon

♯

Thus
March

I looked up and saw
its form
through everything
– it is sewn
in all parts, under
and over

One of the Bronze Plaques Which Decorate These

Shores

> John Hays Hammond Jr
> Yale University graduate
>   Sheffield Scientific 1907
> first user of the super heterodyne
> for directing surface craft
> & later underwater missile
> control

aren't you at least equal to Russia Cement

and Gorton Pew's, Mighty Mac Hammond?

A Letter, on FISHING GROUNDS [of, THE GULF OF MAINE] by Walter H. Rich

If the marine features
of this region are radically different from
those of other coastal bodies of the eastern United States,

so, too, the shore land, battered as it has been by sea and
storm or worn by glacial action or by Arctic currents,

is no less remarkable. No other section of the eastern United
States has a similar coast, so serrated, indented, and ragged,

as has this shore line of the Gulf of Maine. Here the battering
by the forces of nature has resulted in making

thousands of safe harbors and havens
for the navigator. All along shore are strewn

hundreds of islands, a characteristic feature of the region
and one noted with wonder by every early explorer. These

islands, if near the land, are beautiful and smiling; if
in the open sea, of such grandeur; and mainland and island alike

are inhabited by a numerous and hardy race of fisher folk.

The tides within
the Gulf of Maine
have a very great rise and fall as compared with other waters

in this region. At the south
of Cape Cod

tides are seldom over 4 feet in their range, but beginning at
once at the north of Cape Cod with a rise of from 7 to 10
feet these increase quite constantly as they go eastward,
reaching about 28 feet in the neighbourhood of the original
Micmacs, and touch their highest point in Fundy Bay, where
in many places is a rise and fall of 50 feet,

and in some few places tides
of 70 feet are reported. These Indian tides are probably

the greatest in the world. This great ebb and flow of water
serves to aid shipbuilding and the launching of vessels as
well as to carry the deep water far up into the inlets of
the coast and into the mouths of the rivers, making these
navigable for crafts of considerable size well into the
land or up to the lowest falls of the streams.

The climate here
is one of extremes,

and, lying as it does between 42° and 45° north latitude,

the region may be said to be

cold. Apparently the waters of the Gulf of Maine are not affected
by any stray current from the Gulf Stream, which passes at a considerable distance from its mouth – from the mouth of the Gulf of
Maine,   and Brown's Bank – thus doing little to temper the cold
of this area either on land or at sea. Whether these waters are
cooled further by any flow from the Labrador Current may be
questioned. The winters are long,

usually bringing heavy snowfalls, but not now any
longer since the Horse Latitudes have shifted north. Strong gales
used to be frequent during much of the fall and winter time. Perhaps

the most dangerous
of these "blows"

come out of the mountains to the north and northwest of the gulf.
Thus, in addition to the uncertainty of an opportunity to set gear
when once upon the fishing grounds, the winter fishing here is not
without its element of serious danger. While the ice crop in
northern New England never fails, yet,

perhaps because of the strong tidal currents of these glorious waters,
the principal harbors rarely

are closed by ice, or, if closed,
for but a few days only. While the summers

used to be mild and in certain parts of them
extremely hot, fogs are heavy and virtually continuous
during the "dog days" (July 20 to September 1), when southerly
and southwesterly breezes bring the warm moist air from the Gulf
Stream into the cooler currents from the land. The fogs of Fundy

the mists of the Indians
on the land, the flow,
from the ice, of the hidden
speech, the tales they tell
of the m'teoulin, of the masques performed
in the waves, of the Indian watchers making on
to these other men who have come to the shore

the fogs the fogs are especially noted you can walk at night
and read your shadow slanted upward by your side, the tales
the tales to tell in the continuous speech. During the summer seasons

winds from the east and north

bring the only clear weather experienced in the outer chain of
fishing grounds.

'Bahia fonda' – and with my thanks to
R. H. Marchant for letting me keep his
copy of Walter H. Rich, to do this.

Maximus, to Gloucester, Letter 157

an old Indian chief as hant
sat on the rock between
Tarantino's and Mr
Randazza's and scared the piss out of
Mr Randazza so he ran back into
his house

The house I live in, and exactly on the back stairs,
is the sight

of the story
told me by

Mr Misuraca, that,
his mother, reports

that, the whole Fort Section, is
a breeding ground of the ghosts of,

dogs, and that, on those very steps, she saw,
as a girl, a fierce, blue, dog, come at her,

as she was going out, the door

The Tarentines
were the pests

of the coast, a bunch of shore Indians
who raided as far south

as Gloucester, and were themselves conceivably
parts among the Algonquin people

of them there 1000 AD Wikings:
as these Sicilians

talk an Italian
which is Punic. For the Tarantinos

where Micmacs, first spotted off La Have,
and had been dealing,

before they got down here,
as traders with fishermen

since the beginning
of the occupation of the coast

from whom they got
knives and kettles

and coats and then sold them
stolen corn, from peaceful

Indians or shamefully cowardly
Indians who put up with these

Tarentines, huddling in their
shabby huts begging the new-come white man to

help them up against this raiding bunch
of old tough remnants of the older

coast. Or they were dogs, the Tarentinos,
come in to feed on the after coast,

after the white man disease
– the yellowing disease,

the Indians themselves called
what no man yet has diagnosed,

except that Indians,
who had been hauled,

to London,
seem somewhere,

to have brought it
back. These Tarentines

were intrusions
on all the coast, east

of Penobscot Bay

why light, and flowers? Paul Oakley,
directly, from Main Street down Water
over the water
at the other side of the inner harbor

on the other side of

over and above
the masts, looking down on the Older Scene

gardens ran
to the water's
edge (on East-facing appropriated
quarter-plots

I'm looking
at how the Virgin
does dominate
her Hill and place
between the Two Towns

from the East to North fall
of Main, at Water, right angle
Paul Oakley, directly down Main she
in the same direction & picking up the same light

as 90 Middle, the gambrel
which is sliced off,

the shape of light

the lay,
of flowers

Fort Point section

you drew the space in
reticule
now spread the iron net,
Enyalion

Civic Disaster   for Ed Bloomberg

There's a peach tree growing at least
on the Fort though Dutchie
the two dark last old country drest
Sicilian ladies, who sat under it
and under the grape vine, cut their
cherry tree down before Dutchie his
and his apple finally because
some idea of threat that children's
parents would sue – I said have they?
                    He paid $30, and one morning
the dirty whine of an automatic saw
(I thought I was back in the mountains)
woke me the house was in a flap out the window the apple tree
was gone
          So I console myself
in the last spring discovering
that down on the other side of the hill
where Sam Novello who now owns the Federal Fort property proper
throws his rubbish up over the fence by the barking dogs
who yell each time the city Fire Alarm goes off
there is these days this peach tree bravely blooming

best spring yet, 19-
63 (it was Levasseur's
nursery he works for and
drives their truck cut
Dutchie's tree – Bartlett's
Tree Nurses or something like
that, 30 dollars; and Ed
Bloomberg told me weeks later
he wanted me to explain to him
the poem and I said what do
you think and he sd I guess
it means never give up (hope?

Well, his blue eys shown (one
other man I met in Nelson's
pharmacy (haveing an ice cream
cone, has one every afternoon
2:30 two years since his re-
tirement) had em too; and they
are not the fireing aquamarine
eyes of the Devil of half-
lust which burst like four-
footed movement of Nebuchad-
nezzar's tile of the lion
and the bull was it he is
flanking???)

June 6th, 1963

the Head and Chariot
of the Maiden laid
out in gold fillet

With Horsemen
and Senior Citizens
half the size
of the Single Wise Female Body
holding the Saucer up, over their Heads
in the center of the Crowd of them
mounted on the Platform of the 4-Wheeled
Vehicle

Among the 8
24 pounders
on the rampart or bulwark
of the Fort raised on the granite
of the island, or head of the Neck,
sticking out into the Harbour of
Glowceastre

the Head was Chariot
for the Maiden drawn
on the 4-Wheeled Vehicle,
or Cart

By the rock
behind the tenement
beside the Orlandos
the road or entrance – gorge –
to the Fort, by which soldiers
supplies food ammunition guard
whatever was the necessities to
maintain the bastion (properly speaking)

the Exterior Slope
made nearly vertical (already

deviation from grammar of
fortification) was more properly
character of
glacis

the Head of the Maiden layed
in the Fort or Castle

in honor of JOHN WHITE,
of Dorchester, founder
of
the Dorchester Company
(on grounds of
Hanseatic League – Bel-
gae) and directly as of
appeal Conant, Stage
                    Fort,
by letter received,
          "receptacle
for those of religious
purpose to found in
                    this
new country a permanent
settlement", 6 of the
                    90
of the Dorchester Co.
          survived into
the New England Company,
also of Mr. White's
urging and creating

into the hill went into
the hill every Sunday
went through
      the face of the
         mountain

and on the other side
was fucked by
the mountain

the distances

up and down

that the sea

may not rush in   an abatis

to be put around the work   a palisading

be carried across the gorge

Col J G Tottin's

report 1833

Tantrist
sat saw
on the Lingam
of the City
Hall 4 Wheels
Taken off
at each Corner
of the Base of
the City Hall
Tower

I stand up on you, Fort Place

rotundum

the dome
of the City
Fort
defiance
Hill

Or Lindsay
roared upon the town
firing barges,
cutters,
schooners landing parties marines
boarders and those to set fire
to the flake-yards on Pavilion Beach
to let them then ignite the town,

the whole thing to go in flame
and satisfy his whim
because a prize
had driven into Gloucester and ground
on the flats between Pearce's Wharf
and 5 Lb Island

ho-ho sd Captain Englishman
I'll burn the whole town down
meanwhile some musket men
had gathered at the wharf
and killed the 1st 3 Englishmen
who reached the prize's deck,

then Captain Lindsay in his rage
threw balls and balls into the Unitarian
Church, and the other schooner

which he had seized as prize
came in & was equally
retaken as well as 28 marines & assorted
actual English sailors plus

several impressed Americans
in the engagement off Vincent's Cove.

while on Fort Point, or the neck connecting it
to the main, among the fish flakes
where the fellows
from the Falcon
were trying to fire
the flake-yards,

other men of the town
with no trouble at all
gathered up those fellows,

and one of them
had such a short horn
or he was taking such time
trying to set the town on fire,

the combustibles
he had to do it with,
which he had already lit,
curiously enough back right up
very quickly
to his own powder horn
& did blow his hand off

'Tis true two Gloucestermen
did lose their lives

the August day,

and there was fear,

the morning after,

the English sloop-of-war

would surely murder

the defenceless town

but in the morning dawn

lo there the Falcon battleship

in the middle of the harbor

was being warped away

to get a wind and go

out of here

13 vessels, and David Pearce's
Corporal Trim
among them, value of that
cargo 19,000 £ (dollars

and so far as I believe is known
no legislation as of this date yet,
1963, from that period 1794 to 1798,
of a Federal settlement,
    it was a President's Private War

treated as such anyway
any indemnity Gloucester
possibly the sole place
which did suffer damages
from the French
who had supported
the youthful U. States
of America with her Navy
in the previous engagement
of Thomas Jefferson and the
George Washingtons
of the Declaration and the First
War for Independence?

I should imagine
that Federalism
has every right still,
as an objection,
undoing its Stars
and Bars of banking and
collaboration with a South
which does not include Thomas Pinckney
and did Pickering of Salem,
to sit as I did yesterday
in front of the same Library
out of which I regarded City Hall
three days ago and be sure
that a vow one year's long
is now as just a commitment
to a life of the love of God and to do work for others
as it was when the Society of Mercy
was new
        David Pearce
they do say
went broke
    for the last, of four times,
that time due also
to the contemporary loss
of one more cargo
by the maritime law of
port of proposed sale
deviated from
by his captain
unable in storm
to make the entrance mouth

of a tricky river
on the Portuguese shore
of India, or Madagascar,
and was lost trying
to be a Yankee and sell
at another depot

These portions
of a country
which is Northern
and were supported
until Universalism occurred
in Gloucester (the
Tyrian Lodge possibly
was identical with
the Sons of Liberty
the Committee of Correspondence,
for example, was on board Mr. Lindsay's ship
as hostages when the townsmen
of Gloucester did take & retake
the prizes August 8th, 1775
and drove the boarders off Fort Beach,

it is the question of value
which opens again
as though we well were
back in Al 'Arabi's
circumvallum
again right now with
David Pearce's indemnity
not yet paid

I want to open
Mr Oppen
the full inherited file
of history –

that extension
is not satisfactorily
organized

and that order
is for sure art

the heavens above
do declare
the handiwork
of the orbits,

and the axis
of the earth's day,
and the sun's year on earth,
are more important
than the parietal

the societal
is a undeclared war
which, if there are damages,

no matter that the Congress
will not support the President,
the problem then is whether
          a Federal organization
or organization at all except as it comes
directly in the form of
the War of the World
is anything:

      I seize once more
Timothy Pickering as
much which is
what is always wrong

and now say it without any argument
that we are placed
solely on what anyone of us does bring to bear

Written Fort Point
     1st Federally
and effectively fortified
1794-1798,

June 1963

   The total price
lost by the city
in those years was
presented in a bill to the Federal Government of
$200,000

The lap
of the one of the two women who were told
by me, at the water side, to turn around, and be of some help
to get my Father up out of the river,
and Nepthys the queen
of the underground house
wealth (money) is buried
in the hole in the earth
and all I had to do
was scratch with my fingers
and the little people come out
& passed me $1.37¢ worth of change
whenever I wanted it

+++++++++

Directly in front of my own house
(by the choke-cherry tree) at
Stage Fort Avenue. A depression,
in the ground, up hill from the tree
is still there. Or was, the last time
(recently, 1964)
I took my son and daughter
so that they might know
if they wanted to
where to dig

a Contract Entered Into By
the Aforesaid Ship or Vessel Owners of
the Port of Gloucester to
Divide Their Losses By
Agreement to Share Insurance On
Sd Vessels or Ships of Their
Ownership How I Know That
The Dolphin and the Britannia Were
Definitely B. Ellery's Own Owned

Vessels Which the Daily Entries On
His Business of Supplies And
Services Were or Included Obviously

Trips Including A Southern Voyage
Each Year From What Sounded Like
His Back Door at the Green

signed himself B. Ellery Dog Town

The River Map and we're done

by Master Saville who, conceivably, from the accuracy of his drawing of the Fort,
was the Keeper as well as the Drawer
of both the Harbor and the Canal?

wreck here flats Old Bass Rock channel Annisquam
Harbor toll up river Obadiah Bruen's
Island granitite
base river flowing

in both directions ledge only
at one point Rocky Hill and Castle Rock
a few yards further
than Cut Bridge enabling sand
to gather

off mouth
a Table
Rock
like Tablet

a Canal Corporation
to be formed
drawn for the record
of the incorporation

Between Heaven and Earth
kun and on any side Four

directions the banks

and between them River Flowing

in North and South out

when the tide re-

fluxes

carrying a crest
at the mixing point
filling Mill
Stream

at flood immersing
all the distance over

from
Alexander Baker's
goldenrod
field

and dry lavender
field flower guillemot sat and fattened
and the herring gull wasn't even here
mullein aster mustard specularia
knotweed now in the front yard

With the water high no distance
to Sargents houses Apple Row
the river a salt Oceana or lake
from Baker's field to Bonds Hill

nothing all the way
of the hollow of the Diorite
from glacial time to this soft summer night
with the river in this respite solely
an interruption of itself

the firmness of the Two Hills
the firmness of the Two Directions
the bottom of the vase the rise
of the power of the Sea's plant

right through the middle of the River
neap or flood tide

inspissate River
times repeated

old hulk   Rocky Marsh

I set out now
in a box upon the sea

This first edition has been designed, printed, & published by Cape Goliard Press, 10a Fairhazel Gardens, London N.W. 6. Of this edition 100 copies have been numbered, signed by the author, & case-bound. In addition, 26 copies, lettered A-Z, have been signed by the author & specially hand-bound & boxed by A.W. Bain & Co. Ltd., London.

Printed in Great Britain.